Women
IN THE
Bible

Miriam
Mary &
Me

Lois Miriam Wilson

Northstone

Editing: Michael Schwartzentruber and Jim Taylor
Consulting art director: Robert MacDonald
Cover design: Lois Huey-Heck

Permissions:

Mary Mary Quite Contrary, and *Miriam's Story* used by permission of the author, Rose Ferries.

Lessons from Long Ago first appeared in the *United Church Observer* and is used by permission of the author, Donna Sinclair.

At Jacob's Well first appeared in *The Bright and Morning Star,* Cobalt, Ontario: Hightway Bookshop, and is used by permission of the author, Beatrice Arnill.

Martha's Story used by permission of the author, Margaret Joyce

Wise Woman of Abel used by permission of the author, Megumi Matsuo Saunders.

Why Not? used by permission of the author, Jean Little.

Native Nativity and *New Life,* by Gladys Taylor, first appeared in *Spirit of Gentleness.* Used by permission.

Quotations from *In Memory of Her: A Feminist Theological Reconstruction of Christian Origins* by Elisabeth Schussler Fiorenza. Copyright © 1983 by Elisabeth Schussler Fiorenza. Reprinted by permission of The Crossroad Publishing Company.

Quotations from "Images of Women in the Old Testament," in *Religion and Sexism,* Rosemary Radford Ruether ed., New York: Simon and Schuster, used by permission of the author, Phyllis Bird.

Quotation from *Writing a Woman's Life* by Carolyn Heilbrun, W.W. Norton & Company, Inc., used by permission.

Quotation from *The Illegitimacy of Jesus,* by Jane Schaberg, Harper and Row, used by permission.

All materials quoted from World Council of churches publications used by permission of the World Council of Churches, Department of Communication, Geneva, Switzerland.

Most Bible quotations are from *The Revised Standard Version, The Jerusalem Bible,* and *The New English Bible.*

Northstone Publishing Inc. is an employee-owned company, committed to caring for the environment and all creation. Northstone Publishing recycles, reuses and composts, and encourages readers to do the same. Resources are printed on recycled paper and more environmentally friendly groundwood papers (newsprint), whenever possible. The trees used are replaced through donations to the Trees for Canada Program sponsored by Scouts Canada. Ten percent of all profit is donated to charitable organizations.

Canadian Cataloguing in Publication Data

Wilson, Lois, 1927–
    Miriam Mary and Me

ISBN 1–55145–082–8
1. Women in the Bible—Juvenile literature. 2. Bible stories, English.
I. Title.
BS575.W54 1996   j220.9'2   C95–911149–2

ISBN 0–929032–77–2 1st edition, 1992

**Published under license from Wood Lake Books by
Northstone Publishing Inc.**

**Printed in Canada by
Quebecor Printing Inc.**

Dedicated to my grandchildren:

Nora
Annie
David
Meg
Jane
Lois
Murray
Sarah
Stuart

and those still to be born.

Table of Contents

Introduction

Most of the stories told in this book took place a long time ago and in a different culture. Originally, they were told around campfires, memorized, reflected on by the community, embroidered, and then finally, years later, they were written down. Because of this, it is hard to know what the stories meant to their original hearers. And just as significantly, we have to think about what the stories mean for us today.

It is important that we know and read these stories. The characters they portray, while different from us, are also very much like us. Their story is our story. They speak of who we are as a people of God. Their story, and ours, is one of struggle, joy, deceit, shame, triumph, despair, and love.

We find it difficult to understand some of these stories, particularly those about captivity and poverty. Today, people in many parts of the world who are captive or poor can help us understand the struggle in the biblical story. Their comments, and sometimes their stories, have been included. Some stories have a lot of violence in them. We include them, not to commend violence, but to reflect life as it really was and is.

Most Bible stories have been written by men, about men. To balance that point of view, women have begun to read the stories through the lens of women's struggles for justice and wholeness. Some of the stories therefore explore Jesus' attitudes to women. Some stories, like Judith and Deborah, are included because they were strong women. Some women who were not "successful," according to a male-dominated culture, have been included. Among them is the story of Vashti. Some stories are about the expanding scope of women's participation in the ministry of Jesus. Some make links between women's liberation and human liberation.

At no point did we try to whitewash the biblical characters, or make them models of purity fit for the ears of children. The failings and the ugly side of women are presented as well as their triumphs and their beauty. It is important not to betray children by reading to them only the palatable, good things. Their knowledge is beyond their years, and by age five children have posed every theological question that exists, including "Why do people die?" and "Is there a God?"

Some of the stories were written by individuals from different parts of Canada, some by myself, some by groups across this country, and some by women from other countries. In every case, each person has been credited with the story she or he wrote. What becomes essential is that women see themselves collectively as storytellers.

Stories will continue to be written and new interpretations of old stories will continue to find their way into our culture as people wrestle with the biblical text and as the storyteller interacts with the listener.

rooted in the Judaic Christian knowledge of a God who sets people free and who requires justice and mercy, both in the personal and in the public socio-economic political sphere. Stories have been selected to reinforce the Judaic Christian belief that the ultimate test of faithfulness to God is the just and merciful treatment of widows and orphans, strangers, and the poor.

What the stories are

Stories for children
"Whoever receives
one such child in my name
receives me," (Matthew 18:5).

A child's religious experience is valid. Children are not just small adults being groomed for maturity. A child is not an empty vase into which all manner of ideas, morality, good thoughts, and religious options are poured. Stories are to take both children and adults on a journey of self-discovery that will yield rich mutual learnings.

"As of old it was said...
but I say unto you."
The recorded biblical stories remain the basis for these stories, which I have tried to tell in new ways. They are

What the stories are not

Not for every occasion
The stories were not written for church services, nor for Sunday School curriculum, but rather for adults who love to read to children. Most are intended to be read to children on a one-to-one basis, although some of them may be appropriate for reading to larger groups.

Not the usual stories
The stories do not encompass the complete Bible. I have been very selective. Indeed, many of the stories told here have never been understood as central to the story of salvation but have been seen as mere adjuncts to the main action. I have chosen them for this collection because they are stories of women on the margins. Some of them deal with scripture that is not well known to the reader, which is why

I have included background material for the adult.

Not lectionary based

Selections have not been based on the ecumenical lectionary since the lectionary too is an arbitrary ordering of biblical passages by predominantly male theologians. Examination of the lectionary indicates that few of the stories included in this book are included in it.

Not for scholars

This book was not written in academic terms, although scholars will recognize the debt owed to recent feminist scholars (both Jewish and Christian) who have made their unpublished articles and theses freely available, and who have expressed interest in the stories. Special acknowledgment is due the Roman Catholic scholar Elisabeth Schussler Fiorenza, and a religiously observant feminist Jew, Norma Joseph. Responsibility, however, for the final draft is mine alone.

Not geared to a particular age group

The stories are not geared to a particular age group. All of them, however, are thought to be useful to those who read to children on a one-to-one basis. The reader and the child will soon decide what age will resonate to a particular story.

Not an individual effort

Grateful thanks is extended to the McGeachy Scholarship Committee of the United Church of Canada for the opportunity to explore and research theology out of women's struggles as outlined in the McGeachy paper, and for the extension of that research in this Bible story book; to persons and groups across Canada who participated in workshops to develop theological approaches to biblical stories out of women's struggles; to those who actually penned stories, some of which are included in this book; to Lakehead University, Thunder Bay, for the use of a computer; to the children and grandchildren who contributed new shades of meaning; to Jim Taylor and Michael Schwartzentruber for editing, design, and layout; and to my husband Roy, who put up with me "being in the basement" again.

An invitation

The rest of the stories are yet to be written. All this book attempts to do is to point the reader in a particular direction. It is a beginning and an approach. It is, hopefully, a first step and an open door. Readers should try their own hand, and make their own exploration.

Lois Miriam Wilson

Women Who Break Stereotypes of Female Behavior

Women have always faced pressure to conform to the expectations of society. But in all eras, certain women have chosen to establish their identity outside of the traditional roles defined by society. Perhaps, then, this is the best place to begin.

The following stories about Mary and Martha are Christian "midrash," that is, stories *about* Bible stories. Before going any farther, read the suggested scripture.

Traditional interpretation of the Luke story has too often maligned Martha and praised Mary. It has been interpreted in three ways: To teach the value of faith over works; to praise the worthy woman (Mary) over the unworthy woman (Martha busy in the kitchen); or to describe our psychological processes.

Catholic theologian Elisabeth Schussler Fiorenza rejects all three traditional interpretations. The summary of her mind-boggling position (the whole of which you can read in a most interesting article cited below) is that she thinks Martha owned her own home and became one of the first "bishops" of the early faith community. Her preparations for "serving at table" were to do with her role as *diakonos*, as server of the table fellowship we now call communion. Certainly she was *not* making coffee.

The John story presents Martha's stunning confession of faith, of Jesus as "the Christ, the Son of God" (John 11:27). She is also presented as the sister with initiative and assertiveness (John 11:20–21). She calls Mary to come with her (John 11:28).

Mary was one of the early ministers/preachers in the house church. Her role was complementary to Martha's and they both exercised major leadership roles in the early gatherings of Christians. Both women – along with Vashti and Huldah, whose stories we also tell in this section – broke stereotypes of female behavior.

For Further Reading

Fiorenza, Elisabeth Schussler. "A Feminist Critical Interpretation for Liberation: Martha and Mary." In *Religion and Intellectual Life*, Vol. 3 No. 2, Winter, 1986.

Theological Criteria and Historical Reconstruction: Martha and Mary, Luke 10:38–42. Protocol of the 53rd Berkeley California Center for Hermeneutical Studies in Hellenistic and Modern Culture, 1987.

Moltmann-Wendel, Elisabeth. *The Women Around Jesus: Reflections on Authentic Personhood*. London: SCM, 1982.

Mary Mary Quite Contrary
Luke 10:38–42

The mainstream of rabbinic tradition viewed a woman's role as that of wife and mother. This was not understood to be negative or confining within the societal structure of the times.

The greatest good was the fulfilment of God-commanded *mitzvot* in order to preserve the covenant between God and the people. A woman's realm was the law of family purity: *niddah*, the separation of dough to prepare loaves of bread; and *hallah*, the lighting of the Sabbath candles.

The Talmud said that women had no obligation to teach others or themselves, and that others had no obligation to teach them. In a society that believed the intellect to be an instrument of sanctification, and study to be a sanctified act, most women were thus deprived of participation in one of the most hallowed expressions of faith. In fact, most ancient cultures did not encourage girls to read or study.

Rabbinic tradition, however, was capable of recognizing and respecting selected women as sources of Torah. For example, there was the prophet Huldah; the ritualist, Abba Hilkiah's wife; and the scholar Berwiah. No doubt Jesus knew of this tradition and built on it.

For Further Reading

Goldfeld, Ann. "Woman as Source of Torah in Rabbinic Tradition." In *The Jewish Woman*, Elisabeth Kolten ed., New York: Schocken Books, 1976.

Mary Mary Quite Contrary

story by Rose Ferries, Winnipeg, Manitoba

Mary, Mary
Quite contrary,
How does your reading go?

With scrolls and books
In crannies and nooks
And ideas to and fro.

Mary wasn't like the other girls in Bethany. She was quite different.

She looked like the other girls. She had long dark brown hair and smooth olive skin. She had a high sweet voice when she spoke and when she sang. Yes, she looked like the other girls. And she sounded like the other girls.
But she didn't act like them.

THEY liked to play wedding.
Mary wanted to run races with the boys.

THEY wanted to dance. Mary wanted to climb a tree.

THEY helped their mothers in the kitchen so they could learn how to cook. But Mary wanted to learn how to read.

"Read?" said her mother. "Girls don't read!"
"Read?" said her father. "Girls don't read!"
"Read?" said her granny and her aunt and her cousins
and the woman who lived next door.

"Listen Mary! GIRLS DON'T READ!"
But Mary wanted to learn how to read.

Mary began to grow up.

But still Mary wasn't like the other young women in Bethany.

She looked like the other young women. She had long, dark brown hair which she covered now with a scarf. Her olive skin was smooth and her voice when she sang or spoke was high and sweet.

Yes, she looked like the other young women. And she sounded like the other young women. But she didn't act like them.

THEY wanted to dance. Mary wanted to go for long walks.

THEY stayed at home with their mothers, cooking and sewing. But Mary wanted to read.

"Read?" said her mother. "Girls don't read!"
"Read?" said her father. "Girls don't read!"
"Read?" said her granny and her aunt and her cousins and the woman who lived next door.

"Listen, Mary! GIRLS DON'T READ!"

But Mary wanted to read. She wanted to read and study.

Mary grew up.

She learned how to cook. (Although her granny's food tasted better.) She learned how to bake. (Although her aunt's cakes were lighter.) And she learned how to sew. (Although mother's seams were straighter.)

Even though she tried, Mary wasn't like the other women in the village. She wanted to read and study and learn. Everyone tried to talk to Mary.

"Read?" said her mother. "Girls don't read!"
"Read?" said her father. "Girls don't read!"
"Read?" said her granny and her aunt and her cousins and the woman who lived next door.

"Listen Mary! GIRLS DON'T READ!"

But Mary wanted to read and learn and study.

Now Mary's family had a friend named Jesus. One day he was coming to visit them at their home in Bethany. Jesus was a very special friend and they were excited to be seeing him again.
Jesus finally arrived.

"Perhaps," thought Mary, "perhaps I could tell Jesus about wanting to read and study and learn."

So Mary sat and talked to Jesus, about wanting to learn to read, about wanting to study, about how nobody understood, about how when she tried to tell people what she wanted to do they would shout at her.

"Read?" her mother would shout. "Girls don't read!"
"Read?" her father would shout. "Girls don't read!"
"Read!" her granny and her aunt and her cousins
and the woman who lived next door would shout.
"Listen, Mary! GIRLS DON'T READ!"

But Mary wanted to read. She wanted to read and study.

So she told Jesus all that.
And Jesus said:

"Listen carefully to me, Mary. Listen, Mary!
Girls can read.
Girls can study.
Girls can learn."

And so she did.

Martha's Story

This midrash of Martha's childhood lays the groundwork for her adult life of audacious faith, theological astuteness, and courageous activism. It reflects the special relationship Martha had with her brother Lazarus, portrayed in a legend that has both of them adrift on a raft bound for France.

Iconography of the Middle Ages depicts Martha cradling her sick brother Lazarus in her arms during a fierce storm while on the raft.

We do well to remember that legends do not grow up around unexceptional people.

For Further Reading

Weems, Renita, "My Sister's Keeper," in *Just a Sister Away: A Womanist Vision of Women's Relationships in the Bible,* San Diego: Luramedia, 1988.

Martha's Story

story by Margaret Joyce, Ottawa

Her brother was so sickly,
Could neither read nor write
So Martha then began to teach
Her brother, at her side.

Many years ago, outside the town of Bethany, a family lived happily. They were farmers and enjoyed the good things the land produced.

As was the custom, the father spent time with his son Lazarus, preparing him, training him so that one day he would be able to take over the farm.

The mother taught her daughters, Martha, and her little sister Mary, all the things necessary to run and manage a house. The girls learned to sew and dust and clean and cook. They learned what food went on what plates and what foods they could and couldn't eat.

For a time all was well. Lazarus enjoyed playing and laughing with his sisters. Martha, being bright and full of fun, was always able to dream up adventures for them. Mary, the youngest, loved being around her brother and sister, both of whom she idolized.

Now the time came, as it does for all Jewish boys, for Lazarus to go to school. School was held at the synagogue in the center of Bethany. Lazarus enjoyed the classes, especially the friendship of other boys his age. It made it easier to learn, for if the rabbi taught them something that Lazarus didn't understand, he was sure to find one of the other boys who could explain it to him.

Martha and Mary didn't go to school.

One day Martha and Mary were waiting by the gate post for Lazarus to return home. Martha loved to hear about Lazarus' day.

But when Lazarus finally trudged up the lane she noticed how pale and unhappy he looked.

"What's wrong?" Martha asked.

"I'm too slow," complained Lazarus. "I try really hard but I just can't keep up with the other boys any more." And with that Lazarus went inside and lay down before supper.

As the days passed, things didn't get any easier for Lazarus. If anything they got worse. When he got up in the morning he ached in every bone of his body. By the time he got home from the syna-gogue he was pale and feverish and had to go straight to bed.

His parents sent for the doctors. But the doctors couldn't give Lazarus anything to make him feel better. "Rest and time are what is needed," they said.

Lazarus' parents were worried. This was an important year at school for Lazarus. His father went to the rabbi for advice. The rabbi was not sure that Lazarus could do the work but he promised to come out to the farm several times a week to give Lazarus instruction.

"You'll have to help as well," the rabbi told the father. "If we all pitch in, he may be able to do this."

And so it was that the rabbi came out to the farm. Martha sat in the corner and listened. Her quick ear picked up the lyrical rhythms of the language of the Torah. She listened as the rabbi discussed the meaning behind the words. She enjoyed the debate that took place between Lazarus and his teacher.

When the rabbi left, Martha asked Lazarus questions. She wanted him to explain to her what the symbols meant. He was often too tired to show her very much, but before long Martha could read and keep up with the lessons the rabbi gave. The family knew that Martha could do things other girls never learned how to do. The rabbi and her parents soon included her in lessons meant for Lazarus. They knew that she would be able to go over the lessons with Lazarus again and again.

Martha enjoyed this. She doted on her brother, caring for him, nursing him, and when he was well enough, teaching him. The day approached for him to go to the synagogue to read the Torah to the elders. Martha rehearsed it with him. They practiced in the morning and again in the afternoon. She felt sure that he was ready.

Martha wanted to see Lazarus stand at the front of the synagogue. But women were not allowed. They had to stand behind a barrier. The rabbi recognized the family when they arrived. He smiled at her father who stood proudly among the other men. But to Martha the rabbi winked a knowing wink. The rabbi knew that without Martha, Lazarus would not have been there at all.

As the service began, Martha pushed her way to the front of the group of women standing behind the barrier. She might not be allowed to watch, but she wasn't going to miss hearing Lazarus read.

When the service was finished and the family gathered outside the synagogue to congratulate Lazarus, the rabbi made his way over to Martha. "Someday, perhaps girls will also be able to read from the Torah and lead the religious celebrations."

Martha smiled, her mind bursting with the possibilities, her heart brimming over with love. "I want that too," she thought. "I'll be ready!"

The Martha Legend
12th Century France

Together with the pictures of women that limit them to the roles of wife or mother, other images have demonstrated the extraordinary vitality of women. "The motif of Martha the dragon-conqueror, for example, originated in 12th century France... remaining popular until the Reformation." (Elisabeth Moltmann-Wendel, *Humanity in God*, p. 44.)

Pictures of Martha with a dragon appeared in the 15th and 16th centuries in parts of Germany and in northern Italy. Great artists such as Luini and Caravaggio depict this theme, as do many rural altars painted by lesser artists.

There is a stained glass window in the south of France that depicts the major elements of this motif. Martha, the integrated woman, stands in flowing robes, bare feet, her waist bound by a cloth girdle. In one hand she holds a small cross, in the other, a jar of holy water. At her feet lies the dragon, tamed.

The story of Martha taming the dragon with her girdle reminds us of our linkage with the animals, of her vulnerability and non-violent power. She stands in stark contrast to a companion window featuring "St. George the Dragon Killer" which conforms to a more violent concept of life and the world.

The new element in the Martha legend is that it is not an armed man who conquers the dragon and who is hailed as a hero and a saint. It is a woman!

Battle with a dragon is a theme found in all mythologies. A monster, from either land or sea, threatens the inhabitants of a village or city with utter extinction. The dragon reminds us of the ever present dark, evil side of human nature, and of all that corrupts and destroys human life. Dragons and leviathans can be found in the Bible, as it tells the story of sin and death being transformed into salvation and life. Here is one such story.

For Further Reading

Moltmann-Wendel, Elisabeth and Jurgen Moltmann. "Martha, A Forgotten Medieval Tradition." In *Humanity in God*, New York: Pilgrim Press, 1983.

The Martha Legend

adapted from Jurgen Moltmann and Elisabeth Moltmann-Wendel, "Martha, A Forgotten Medieval Tradition," in *Humanity in God*

Martha was a leader, Full of love and power,
Martha tamed a dragon, In just one hour!

Many years ago, a great fire-breathing dragon roamed the countryside of France. It had teeth like swords. It was fatter than an ox and stood higher than a horse. The dragon destroyed everything in its path – houses, trees, plants, rivers, caterpillars, birds, insects, apples, people, everything! The people were very afraid of the dragon. They knew only one woman in the village who could stop the dragon. She was very wise and brave. She had cradled her brother Lazarus in her arms when he was sick. She had helped her sister Mary stop crying when Lazarus died. And when Jesus was praying in the garden just before he was crucified, so the story goes, she had stayed awake to watch with him, although all of Jesus' disciples fell asleep.

She wore a long flowing purple robe, with a pure white cloth belt. She never wore shoes because she liked the feel of the grass on her feet and of the sand between her toes. She always carried two things with her: a small cross, and a small jug of water.

The village people trusted Martha to deliver them from the wicked dragon. She felt sad for the people. She thought and thought about what to do. First she thought of drowning the dragon in the sea. Then she thought of burying him in the snow. Finally, she decided that killing the dragon was not the thing to do. She decided to tame him instead.

So one day she went searching for the dragon. She found him

deep in the forest. When the dragon saw her coming, he was angry and spewed fire at her. But Martha held the small cross before his eyes and sprinkled some of the water from her jug on him, and the fire didn't burn her. In fact it stopped burning altogether. The dragon just stood there.

Then Martha took the white cloth belt from around her waist and wound it around the dragon's snout. She wore no armor and used no spear. As she wound the belt around him she patted him tenderly and whispered quietly to him that his fire could be used for the village people, not against them. And when she stroked and polished his scales so that they glowed in the sun, he lay down at her feet, as quiet and tame as a little lamb.

Later, because the dragon had remained quiet for so long, she removed her belt from around the dragon's mouth.

"What do you want me to do?" asked the dragon.

"I'm not sure, but I will ask the people of the village," said Martha.

When Martha returned to the village with the dragon she asked the people, "What do you want the dragon to do?"

"We want the dragon to help us. He can breathe fire into our homes to give us heat to cook our food and keep us warm during the cold winters. We will gladly care for him, if he will care for us in this way."

And so it was. As time passed, the dragon and the people of the village came to accept each other. The dragon no longer hated the village people and the village people no longer feared the dragon.

The villagers collected money and hired one of their best glassmakers to make a beautiful stained glass window for the village church. It showed Martha in her purple cloak and pure white belt, holding her jug of water and the small cross, and the dragon lying peacefully at her feet. You can still see the window today if you visit this church in the south of France.

No Way (Vashti)
Esther 1:1–2:4

The entire book of Esther is a tale written when the Hebrews were dominated by Persia and were in danger of cultural and religious extinction. Chapter 1:1–2:4 focuses on Queen Vashti. At the time, ethnic minorities were forced to assimilate into the dominant Gentile culture. Part of the original intent of the story was to explain the origins of the Feast of Purim which celebrates the resistance of the Hebrews to assimilation.

Two women play the classic bad girl (Vashti) good girl (Esther) roles. Traditionally, Esther's willingness to risk her position and her life for the good of her people has been honored, even though it meant the danger of temporary assimilation of her people into the dominant Gentile culture. Vashti, who defends herself and refuses to demean herself as a woman, is banished from the realm.

Begin by reading the story for yourself. As it opens, the Persian King is giving a lavish banquet for his friends, with much feasting and drinking. When the discussion turns to bragging about whose women were more beautiful, the king decides to display his wife. When Vashti refuses, she is seen to be resisting patriarchal expectations. The king's advisers say she should be banished at once because her unchallenged defiance will seriously undermine their authority! So for the solidarity of the brotherhood, Vashti is banished.

In rabbinic commentaries, Vashti, though "righteous," is maligned and thought to be arrogant. She was so cruel, reads one commentary, that she even forced Jewish maidens to spin and weave on the Sabbath. The patriarchal tradition made sure that the underlying message for women was clear: don't be assertive or disobedient like Vashti, or you'll be a social outcast. Few Jewish children today dress up as Vashti during Purim.

Theology out of women's struggles sees Vashti differently. She had pride, dignity and independence of spirit. She is a strong role model for girls. Her disobedience was her crowning virtue. Nor is this just a judgment out of North America. South African theologian Itumeleng Mosala claims that African feminists identify closely with Vashti. They see her in a positive light and disapprove of those who used her revolt as a means to replace her with a more acceptable queen.

For Further Reading

Gendler, Mary. "The Restoration of Vashti." In *The Jewish Woman*, Elisabeth Kolten ed., New York: Schocken Books, 1976.

Joseph, Norma. Lectures at El-Emmanuel Temple. Toronto, 1991.

Mosala, Itumeleng J. "The Implications of the Text of Esther for African Women's Struggle for Liberation." In *Journal of Black Theology in South Africa*, Atteridgeville, South Africa, Vol. 3 No. 2, November 1988.

No Way (Vashti)

"There's no reason," says Queen Vashti,
"when I say no, to get so nasty."

I wish I could have said, "No way."

But I couldn't. I'm only a young servant in the court of the King of Persia and his Queen Vashti.

The king liked to take guests on tours of the royal gardens that stretched for miles. He loved to show them the alabaster pillars and couches of silver and gold set in a floor of mother-of-pearl and turquoise. But he wouldn't mention the long hours we slaves worked to build his huge palaces.

Once, he gave a great banquet for the nobles and princes which lasted six months! I should know. My father had to cook most of the food, and I had to keep the wine jugs filled. That's hard for a nine-year-old! When they were full, some people waved the food away and said, "No way!" But a lot of people ate too much and had stomach aches, or drank too much and couldn't stand up by themselves. It was a pretty wild party.

When that was over, the king gave another huge feast that lasted seven days. It was for all the people of the city, including us, all our poor friends, and even some of the Israelites who were nothing more than slaves. It was held in the garden court. The wine flowed freely. Believe me, I know because I had to pour it. At the same time, Queen Vashti was giving a banquet for women in the palace. She was saying "Yes, yes," to more food and more music and more dancing. But she was glad to have a separate banquet for the women. She didn't want to be part of the drunken noisiness of the men.

By the last day of his banquet the king was very drunk. He ordered seven of his servants (not me, thank goodness) to bring Queen Vashti before him. He wanted to show off her ravishing beauty to the officers. Everybody knew she was a woman of exquisite beauty.

But to everyone's surprise, Queen Vashti said "No way." She refused to obey the king's command.

One of my friends said it was because she didn't want to display her beauty in front of a bunch of drunken men. They didn't know their right hand from their left, they were so drunk. Others said it was because she was afraid the men would rape her. Another said the king had asked her to wear her royal crown without a veil. One said he had asked her to appear naked except for her crown! Rumor in the palace had it that she was furious, and cried, "I am not my husband's property. No way." When the king heard her reply, he was as mad as hops. His face became red and he began to sweat. He ran around his throne, stamped his feet, and held his head in his hands. Then he summoned his seven princely advisers:

Carshena, Admatha, Tarshish, Shethar, Meres, Marsena, and Memucan. For short I call them C.A.T.S. and the 3 M's. They were used to making rules for the kingdom and they sat on magnificent chairs right next to the king.

"What does the law say must be done with Queen Vashti for disobeying the command of her king?" the king asked. "She says she is not my property. No way, she says. No way indeed. What an insult to me, her master."

CATS and the 3 M's knew that no one would listen to them any more if Vashti got her way.

"Queen Vashti has done wrong," they said, "not to the king alone, but to all the people and officers in the kingdom. Every woman in Persia will say to her husband, 'No way.' There will be endless trouble. Let a royal decree go out, and let it be written in the unchangeable laws of the Medes and Persians, that Vashti shall never again appear before the king. Give her place to a woman who will obey your commands. Give it to someone who will fit into the way things are. When such a law is made public in the land, then all the women will obey their husbands without question."

I thought it was a foolish piece of advice the princes gave the king. There was no way all the women of the land would obey their husbands without question, no matter what the king decreed. But then nobody takes my advice, I'm only a kid.

The king did as CATS and the 3 M's suggested. Vashti was sent away from the court, never again to be Queen of Persia. The law that every man was to be master in his own house was made known all across the land.

I'm too young to say "No way" to that, but wait till I grow up!

I'm Proud (Huldah)
2 Kings 22:1–20

Huldah is one of four prophetesses identified in Hebrew Scripture. The other three are Miriam, who prophesied during the Exodus, Deborah, one of the "judges" who unified the tribes, and Noadiah (Nehemiah 6:14). Huldah, from her "house of study" in Jerusalem, publicly spoke the word of God to announce the fall of Judah, thus bringing the monarchy and that dynasty to an end. Yet this story has traditionally emphasized King Josiah and ignored Huldah.

Josiah was certainly a righteous king. The story, set in 621 BCE, expresses his attempts to cleanse Judean worship of foreign elements and to recall his people to their distinctiveness. The restoration of the temple and his summoning the people for a ceremony of covenant renewal were highlights of his reign. He also ordered the long neglected feast of the Passover to be reinstituted (2 Kings 23:22–23).

Huldah was central to this renewal. She was asked by King Josiah's priests to verify the contents of a law scroll discovered in the Jerusalem temple and believed to contain much of the book of Deuteronomy. Huldah not only attested to the authenticity of the document, but also warned of the "desolation and curse" Yahweh would bring upon Jerusalem if the people continued to disobey their traditional religious laws.

Traditional interpretation of this text emphasizes the goodness of Josiah and the importance of finding the core of the book of Deuteronomy (chapters 12–26) which had been lost.

The biblical text tells us little about Huldah, save the names of her husband, her father-in-law, and his father! Yet she is identified as a prophetess and is consulted by the king ahead of no less a prophet than Jeremiah. To balance the record, we tell the story from Huldah's, or rather her child's, viewpoint.

The traditional role of the woman was to enable her husband to study the Torah, and to begin to educate the young sons at home. The woman herself was under no obligation to study. Huldah was a woman of God who broke the traditional mold and assumed equal prophetic power with males. Huldah's story reminds us that the Judaic tradition was capable of recognizing and respecting female scholars and seers, and that women were not always content to suppress their ability to think and speak publicly.

The narrator of the biblical text appears to implicitly accept the existence of an influential female prophetess as a matter of course. This suggests that significant female leaders may have been more numerous in ancient Israel than the explicit biblical record suggests. Indeed, the Talmud, the written and oral religious tradition, identifies eight prophetesses: Miriam, Deborah, Hannah, Ruth, Abigail, Huldah, Noadiah, and Esther.

The rabbis, while recognizing Huldah's intellectual capacities, had trouble with women prophesying publicly. In *The Legends of the Jews*, Louis Ginzberg quotes a rabbinic source: "This unpleasant feature of her character is indicated by her ugly name – weasel."

The image of self-confidence projected by Huldah challenged rabbinic concepts of womanhood. The telling of this story may enhance the self-image and confidence of young girls.

For Further Reading

Ginzberg, Louis. *The Legends of the Jews*. Philadelphia: Jewish Publication Society, 1912, vol. 6, p. 377.

Goldfeld, Ann. "Woman as Source of Torah in Rabbinic Tradition." In *The Jewish Woman*, Elisabeth Kolten ed., New York: Schocken Books, 1976, p. 259.

Joseph, Norma. Lecture at El-Emmanuel Temple, Toronto, 1991.

Kuzmack, Linda. "Aggadic Approaches to Biblical Women." In *The Jewish Woman*, Elisabeth Kolten ed., New York: Schocken Books, 1976.

Laffey, Alice L. *An Introduction to the Old Testament*. Philadelphia: Fortress Press, 1988, p. 139.

I'm Proud (Huldah)

It's a pain having a famous mother. Nobody ever calls me by name. They just say "Huldah's child did this, and Huldah's child that...." Sometimes I dream of moving miles away from Judah, where no one has ever heard of my mother.

But that might not work either. My father Shallum says that everyone in this part of the world knows my mother Huldah. Even the rabbis. They call her "the weasel," because they're jealous, but they know her.

Why were they jealous? It happened this way.

We lived near the temple. We kids knew it wasn't in very good shape because we played in the courtyard even though it was full of weeds and thistles. The temple's roof sagged and some of the huge stones that used to make the walls had fallen into the courtyard and broken into pieces. It was a mess. Nobody cared. Except King Josiah. He was one of the best kings Judah ever had, my mother used to say as she lit the Sabbath candles.

One day we went as usual to play in the temple courtyard, even though mother had forbidden it. I was playing King Josiah. The stones made a perfect throne.

Then, out of nowhere, a workman appeared.

"Get lost," he snarled. "This isn't a playground. We have too much work repairing the temple to be bothered by a couple of boys."

That night, when I told my father what had happened, he agreed with the workmen.

"It's true," he said. "King Josiah has appointed his secretary Shaphan to be in charge. And he has told Hilkiah the high priest to take the money collected from the people and pay the carpenters, the builders, the masons and the other workmen. It's about time too. That temple is a mess."

A few nights later, Ezra, one of my best friends, and I were playing around the courtyard in the evening when nobody was around. We knew we shouldn't have been there, but it was absolutely the best place to play. We were playing "repairing the temple." We were prying loose the heavy stones that lay in the courtyard, and trying to pile them up to make a make-believe temple. Suddenly, Ezra called me over to his corner.

"Hey I've found a treasure. It's a scroll of some sort. Maybe it's important. Your mother teaches the law to the elders. She knows about these things. I think we should take it home to her."

"We can't!" I cried. "If we do, she'll know we've been playing here when we weren't supposed to."

"Well, give it to your father. He'll know what to do with it."

And so the book of the law, for that is what we had discovered, found its way into the hands of Hilkiah the high priest. Hilkiah gave it to Shaphan the secretary, who read it himself and then read it to the king. The sound of the king's grieving and wailing were heard all through the palace. He knew that his people had not kept the covenant laws of God written in the book.

The following day, the king sent five men – Hilkiah the high priest, Shaphan the secretary, and three others – to visit my mother where she taught and explained the law to the community.

The news of what she said spread like fire.

"Tell the man who sent you to me," she said to the five men, "Thus says the Lord. This is the end of the line of Josiah for the land of Judah. The people have left God, and have become wicked. None of Josiah's sons, or their sons, will ever rule Judah. It is the end. But because King Josiah grieved and wailed when he heard the words of the book of the covenant, and because he decided to keep the covenant, God will pity him. He will die before the land of Judah comes to an end. He will be spared seeing its fall. For he is a good man."

I knew it wasn't a popular message. What I didn't know was that my mother wasn't popular either. At least not among the rabbis. I overheard some of them talking about her the next day.

As usual, Ezra and I were playing where we weren't supposed to play.

"Sh-h-h," whispered Ezra. "I heard one of the rabbis mention your mother's name."

We pressed our ears to the wall and then peeked around the corner.

"...maybe Jeremiah gave her permission to receive the king's messengers," one rabbi was saying.

"She is too proud," ventured a handsome rabbi. "I bet her nose sticks up in the air four inches higher than anyone else's. Why doesn't she just mind her own business like the other women?"

"Did you notice how she began her prophecy? She said, 'Say to the man who sent you to me....' She should have said, 'Say to King Josiah...' She didn't even call him by name," complained a rabbi with the hairs sticking out of his nose.

"Well I'll tell you a name that suits her," said another. "It's an ugly name, because I think it is an ugly thing for her to weasel in and teach the religious law. I nickname her 'weasel.' The only reason Josiah ever heard of her was because her husband is well known."

I was so mad at them. This was my mother they were talking about. I stumbled home, half crying. My father told me not to listen to them.

"Your mother," he said, "is a spiritual leader of our community. She is known as a brilliant woman, a teacher of the sacred law. She is able to help our people and our king understand the Torah. She is a prophetess like Miriam and Deborah. She is my wife. She is your mother. Be proud of her. There aren't many women like her."

It may be a pain to have such a famous mother. But secretly, I was proud of her.

And I still am.

Unconventional Women

Some unconventional Hebrew women, however, expressed themselves and their faith through lifestyles and in contexts that were seen as less than honorable, and sometimes even outlawed, by the culture: prostitution and fortunetelling to name two. (These stories are presented, not as morality tales, but as examples of the unconventional lives some women lead.)

The first two women whose stories are told in this section (Rahab, and the Fortuneteller of Endor) fall within this category. The other women whom we present here are also unconventional, either by virtue of the status they held within society (the Wise Woman of Abel; and Joanna, a woman with access to Herod's court), or in the audacious way they expressed their faith (the woman who anointed Jesus).

Rahab
Joshua 2:1–21; 6; Matthew 1:5; Hebrews 11:31; James 2:25

Rahab is one of four women mentioned in the genealogy of Jesus (Matthew 1:5). She is a prostitute, named in Hebrews 11:31 as a "saint" justified by her faith, and in James 2:25 as justified by her deeds. The longest account of her story is found in Joshua 2:1-21 and the sequel in Joshua 6. Read all these references before proceeding any further.

Do not think of Rahab as different from people today. There are many modern parallels. Rahab, for example, hung a red cloth out her window to protect herself and her family from the attacking forces. In much the same way, says a Korean woman involved in the student riots in South Korea a few years ago, informants among the students wore black gloves, to protect themselves from being beaten by riot police.

An Asian woman has written that Rahab reminds her of Philippine prostitutes today. They will do anything for their families. The story in Joshua 2 tells how Rahab negotiated for her family's security with her Israelite conquerors. So many women in the Philippines are engaged in prostitution precisely for the security of their families – fathers, mothers, sisters, brothers, and even daughters. One family of eight that I met in Thailand was supported by the money earned by their two daughters, who were prostitutes in Bangkok. The daughters and the family had no other choice or option. Like them, Rahab's virtue was that she was willing to do what was possible and what was needed for the sake of her family and her extended family, "all who belonged to her."

She was a foreign woman to the Israelites and one of considerable independence. She owned her own house and was able to make a binding promise without recourse to any man. She was obviously resourceful and used to hiding men on short notice!

The major action in the book of Joshua is the occupation of the land of Canaan by the Israelites. After they crossed the Jordan River they set about taking the land. The city of Jericho was first on their list. Here is the story of a foreigner and a prostitute whose decisive action is critical to the first successful taking of the land. Perhaps we can understand Rahab's action for her family when we reflect on what our own family means to us.

Rahab

Rahab let the men down,
Showed a scarlet cord.
Saved herself and family,
From a death by sword.

Thump Thump Thump.

The knocking on the door sounded angry.

Thump Thump Thump.

"You in there. Open up in the name of the king!"

Trembling, I opened the door just a crack. Two of the king's guards peered down at me. They wore full armor and had swords belted to their waists.

"Where is the woman of the house? Bring her to us," they demanded.

What had Auntie Rahab done now I wondered. I was scared for her but I knew I had no choice. I whirled around and ran back into the house.

"Auntie Rahab! Auntie Rahab!"

Auntie came down from upstairs and said "It's all right child, I can handle this." Then she went to the door. I pressed myself into the corner behind the door and listened.

"Two enemy spies came to your house last night and are still here," the guards stated. "Bring them out."

Many people thought my aunt was a bad woman. There were men going in and out of her house day and night. Some of them stayed the night with her, though she wasn't married. She never told anyone their names. But this was different. Spies! They must be Israelites – foreigners and enemies of the king. Auntie Rahab was really in trouble now.

"Yes, they came to my house late last night," Auntie said, "but I threw them out shortly after they arrived. I don't know where they went. If you hurry after them, you might catch them." She pointed outside the city gate.

The king's men made their horses gallop down the road outside the city, and the gates were closed as soon as they had left.

I couldn't believe my ears. Auntie had lied. Now I knew who the soldiers were looking for. Last night I had taken two men to the roof of the house. Auntie Rahab had hidden them among the stocks of flax which she kept there. As far as I knew, the men were still there.

"Why did you tell the guards that silly story?" I asked. "And why did you hide the spies last night?"

"You've found me out, have you?" She grinned at me. "All right Rachel, I'll tell you. You're old enough. Come with me."

We climbed the stairs to the roof of the house and found the men still hiding amongst the flax. Auntie Rahab told them that she knew they were strong fighters, and that our city of Jericho would soon be captured by their armies.

Auntie Rahab and I both knew what that meant. Everyone would be killed, including our family. But Auntie Rahab didn't say this to the spies. She didn't tell them that we both knew that the fall of Jericho would mean death to us and our family. I felt like a mouse chased by a cat. I felt trapped. But not Auntie Rahab. She started to bargain with the spies.

"I love my family and friends very much," she said. "I have hidden you from the king's soldiers and saved you from death. In return, when you conquer the city, spare the lives of my father, my mother, my sisters, and my brothers and all who belong to us."

"We will do as you ask if you do not give us away to the king's men," the spies replied. "You have been good to us. When we conquer this city, we will spare you and your family from death."

"You must get out of this house secretly and as soon as possible," she warned. "Your lives are still in danger."

"I know a way Auntie," I said excitedly. "The window at the back which faces the alley. It's just big enough for a man to climb in or out. I've played in it lots of times."

"Good girl!" said Auntie Rahab. Then she turned to the men.

"Are you willing to try it? You'll have to squeeze. The opening is small."

They nodded their heads yes. Auntie got a rope and tied it to a stone in the opposite wall. She gave the other end of it to each man in turn, and lowered them down to the ground through the narrow opening.

One of the men was so fat I thought he'd get stuck. But he didn't. I heard his feet hit the ground.

Auntie and I ran downstairs and out the door. Then we sneaked around to the back alley. "Take to the hills and hide there," she said to the spies, "or you will be caught. The king's men will stop looking in a couple days and then you can go on your way."

Before they left the spies warned her that they could not keep their part of the bargain unless she did exactly what they told her.

"Before we return," they warned, "fasten a piece of scarlet cord to your window. Have the little one here help you get everybody together in the house – your father, your mother, your brothers and sisters, yourselves – your whole family. If anybody goes outside your house, it will be at their own risk. If anyone tries to hurt the people in your house, we will protect you."

I breathed a sigh of relief.

"But remember," they warned, "if you don't keep your end of the bargain, we won't keep our promise either."

I became anxious again. I started sweating.

"If I don't hang the scarlet cord from the window, you won't protect us," Auntie repeated. "Have I understood you correctly?"

"That's it," they said.

"Then I'll do it," Auntie said in a firm voice.

I was glad to see the men leave.

"Let's go and hang the cord right now Auntie," I urged.

We scrambled upstairs and fastened the cord in the window just as the men told us to. My stomach was still in knots with fright. Then Auntie said to me, "Go and tell my father, my mother, my sisters and brothers, my friends, and all our family to come here. Go quickly."

Three days later it happened. The Israelites attacked and the city of Jericho fell. We watched for the two spies night and day. Finally they came. They brought all of us to safety outside the city as they said they would. Then they set fire to the city and everything that was in it. It was terrible. Only Auntie Rahab and those close to her were spared.

That's why I'm still alive to tell you the story.

The Fortuneteller of Endor
1 Samuel 28

This story is about a woman who was a medium, a fortuneteller, a diviner. Such folk have always been considered "on the edge." Even today, they are viewed with disbelief, amusement, or derision. Yet many people consult them, believing them to have special insights and gifts.

The incident in this story took place at the end of King Saul's reign. King Saul was facing a battle and had been trying to determine the battle's outcome against the enemy Philistines, but without success.

After Samuel died, Saul had expelled the mediums, fortunetellers, and wizards from the land. They were part of a peripheral, banned religious system. But in desperation, Saul asked his servants to find him a woman who was a medium. He still had some faith in them.

When his servants reported the existence of a woman at Endor who was a medium, Saul disguised himself to visit her, since he was her announced enemy.

When the medium brought up the spirit of Samuel, she described him as "a ghostly form coming up out of the earth." According to Jo Ann Hackett, writing in *The Women's Bible Commentary*, the dead themselves were often believed to be divine. Not only was Samuel called divine by the medium, but he was also expected to have knowledge of the future battle, knowledge that would ordinarily belong in the divine realm.

After making contact with the deceased Samuel, the woman slaughtered the fatted calf, baked cakes, and served them to Saul and his men. The verb "to slaughter" can also mean "to slaughter as a sacrifice."

It is particularly significant that Saul participated in a sacrificial meal prepared by this female diviner as part of her clerical function in a marginalized and banned religious system. Being a woman, she would have been excluded from the all-male hierarchy of the traditional liturgies, but she was famous enough to have been known by Saul's servants. In any case, she was one of the few women of the religious community who is recorded as having exercised public power.

This story is one of three in the book of Samuel about women wielding public power – the other two being the "wise" women of Tekoa (2 Samuel 14) and of Abel (2 Samuel 20). Both stories assume that the women had public authority and status, a marked contrast to most women whose activities were confined to the home.

For Further Reading

Hackett, Jo Ann. "1–2 Samuel." In *The Women's Bible Commentary*, Carol Newsom and Sharon H. Ringe eds., Westminster/John Knox Press, 1992.

The Fortuneteller of Endor

There was a woman of Endor,
Who helped King Saul by night,
She told him all that Samuel said,
How Saul would lose the fight.

She killed the fatted calf,
She baked a little cake,
And frightened Saul enjoyed it all,
And never thought her fake.

Many years ago I lived in Endor. People used to come from miles around to ask me about the future. They wanted to know if they would be rich or poor, who they would marry, or how many children they would have, if they would die young from illness, or be healthy and live to old age.

One night, after dark had fallen, three men came to my door. The tallest of the three asked me, "Are you the one they call the witch of Endor?"

"I am she," I whispered. My tongue stuck to the roof of my mouth. I was scared.

"Will you tell me my fortune by asking the dead? Will you call up the man I name to you?"

I shook with fright.

"Surely sir," I whispered, "you know what King Saul has done, how he killed some fortunetellers and ordered the rest out of the country. I'm not supposed to live here. Why do you force me to do what will lead to my death?"

"As God lives, no harm will come to you," the tall man promised.

I'm not sure why, but I believed him. When I asked the name of the dead person he wished me to call up he said, "Samuel."

I started trembling again. Samuel had been a great prophet. Who was I to try and speak to such a prophet. And yet it seemed I had no choice. I lit my candles and in my mind I called to Samuel. When I saw Samuel appear, I screamed in fright. I knew at once that my tall visitor was King Saul. He had put on old clothes so nobody would recognize him. But it was him all right.

"You have tricked me," I shouted at him. "You are Saul!"

"Do not be afraid," Saul said to me. "Nobody will harm you. Just tell me what you see. What is my future?"

So I told him what I saw. It was a ghostly figure coming up from the earth.

"What is it like?" he wanted to know.

"Like an old man," I answered, "wrapped in a cloak."

We both knew it was Samuel. Saul bowed low with his face to the ground.

Then Samuel said to Saul, "Why have you disturbed me? What

do you want to know?"

"I am in great trouble," said Saul. "The Philistines are coming against me in battle. God no longer answers me through the prophets or through dreams. I don't know what to do. Can you tell me?"

Samuel answered, "Why do you ask me, now that God no longer answers you? You have not been loyal to God so God has given the kingdom to another man, David. The Philistines will win the battle. Tomorrow, you and your sons will all be dead."

Saul fell to the ground. He was sweating. His eyes grew big with fear. He started to roll around the floor and moan and hold his head in his arms.

I said to him, "I risked my life to obey you. I listened to you. Now you listen to me." I knew it was the king I was talking to, but he needed someone to help him. He might be killed tomorrow, but tonight he was still my king.

"Let me feed you a little. You need strength to stand up and go home," I said. I often did this as part of a forbidden religious ritual to give strength to people who consulted me. I was one of a few women who did this secretly. If people found out we would have been killed for sure.

At first, Saul refused to eat anything. Maybe he was afraid to take part in the ritual because he himself had banned it from his kingdom. But his two servants urged him to eat. Finally he got up and sat on my couch. I had a fatted calf, so I quickly butchered it and cooked it. I took some flour, kneaded it and baked unleavened cakes for the sacrificial meal. Then I set the food before Saul and his servants and they ate it!

They left that same night, as secretly and as quietly as they had come. I've never seen them since.

The Wise Woman of Abel
2 Samuel 20:14–22

We have all heard of the great King David. Few of us have heard the stories of the women who saved him from disaster and death – Abigail, Michal, or the unnamed wise woman of Abel. Here we tell the story of that unnamed woman.

This woman exercised public power in a culture that confined most women to the domestic sphere. She was a "wise" woman, known for her astute counsel, persuasiveness and tact. "Wisdom" was a gift like prophecy, honored and sought after.

When Joab, David's general, besieged the city of Abel and attacked it in order to drive out the one man he wanted to kill (the rebel Sheba who had taken refuge there), a wise woman from within the city asked to speak with him. Joab listened to her, indicating that perhaps she held a public office that Joab recognized, and that she was respected and known far beyond her own city. She negotiated for the lives of the people of Abel by agreeing to turn over the rebel (or rather, his head!) to Joab. When Joab suggested that she get the people's permission to give Sheba up the woman agreed to do so. She convinced the people that Sheba's head was less a loss to them than their lives or their city. She carried out the agreed plan. Sheba's head was delivered and the attack was called off.

Although she is the key player, this wise woman guiding a city's destiny remains unnamed. This reinforces her unimportance in the eyes of the traditional reader. But for us, the astonishing thing about this story is that it depicts a woman clearly representing all the people of the city. They listen to her in matters of war and politics. Her authority is also recognized by Joab, a national figure.

Some will question why we include the story of a woman who cuts off her enemy's head. You remember that David cut off Goliath's head and is revered as a hero for that. This woman acted with the same courage. Only after **both** stories have been told can one raise the question of the morality of cutting off the head of one's enemy.

For Further Reading

Hackett, Jo Ann. "1–2 Samuel." In *The Women's Bible Commentary*, ed. Carol Newsom and Sharon H. Ringe, Westminster/John Knox Press, 1992.

Laffey, Alice L. "An Unnamed Wise Woman." In *An Introduction to the Old Testament – A Feminist Perspective*, Philadelphia: Fortress Press, 1988.

The Wise Woman of Abel

adapted from a story by
Megumi Matsuo Saunders, Winnipeg

A woman of Abel was wise
In counseling some compromise
She cut off Sheba's head
So her enemies fled
Thus she saved that city of Abel.

Leah, a nine-year-old girl, was visiting her grandmother when the trouble began.

"Grandma did you hear something?" she asked. A sudden wave of sound made her shiver with fright. She ran to stand beside her grandma.

"Yes I did, Leah."

Leah heard men shouting. Her throat was dry with fear. She grasped her grandma's hand tightly.

"Hang on tightly Leah. We must go and see what is happening," said her grandma.

Outside, the streets were crowded with people. Leah and her grandma forced their way to the city wall. Everywhere, people were running and shouting.

"Watch out! An army is outside our city wall. We are surrounded. War! War!"

Leah smelled the enemy soldiers' horses and heard them neighing. She heard scraping noises as the attacking soldiers dug tunnels and built ramps—anything to get inside the walls of the city. One of the head men was shouting at the top of his lungs.

Leah's wise grandma was respected by all the people of the city. "Why are they doing this? What should we do?" she thought to herself. Her grandma loved the city very much and knew she had to do something. She prayed for wisdom and courage in the words of the prophet Isaiah, "O God, you who have carried us in your womb from the beginning, carry and save us now." Then she climbed up on the city wall where she could see the attacking army. Of course the soldiers could see her too. So could Leah, who scrunched down behind the wall.

Leah's grandma shouted, "Listen! Listen!" Everyone was quiet.

"Listen! Listen!" she cried again, her voice so firm and clear that everyone could hear. Leah's heart almost stopped beating. She prayed softly, "Please God, help my grandma."

"Tell Joab, your General, to come here. I want to speak with him," Leah's grandma demanded.

Joab, who had been a general for King David for a long time, came forward.

"Are you Joab?"

"Yes I am," he answered. A hush fell on the crowd.

"Listen to me sir," Leah's grandma announced with confidence. "Long ago people used to say that Abel was a great city, one of the most peaceful and loyal in all of Israel. Why do you come with an army to capture it? Why do you want to destroy our city? Do you want to ruin what belongs to God?"

Leah thought she would faint, waiting for Joab's reply.

"Never, never," he called out. "I will never destroy this city. That is not my plan."

"Then why is your army building ramps and digging under our city wall?"

"A worthless fellow, Sheba, started a rebellion against King David," shouted Joab. "He and some of his followers are hiding in your city. Hand over this one man and we will leave your city in peace."

Leah was so relieved to hear what Joab said that she started to cry.

"Very well," shouted Grandma quickly. "We will throw Sheba's head over the wall to you." Then she went to the people of the city with her plan.

"It a wise plan," remarked one.

"It will save the lives of all the people of the city," said another.

So Leah's grandma ordered that Sheba's head be cut off and thrown over the wall to Joab.

"Listen! I hear trumpets!" cried Leah in delight. She knew that the sound of trumpets meant that Joab's army was leaving.

"Grandma, you have saved the city. I am proud of you."

My Mother's Vow
Judges 13

Start by reading this story in Judges 13. It tells of Samson's birth. It precedes the story of Samson as a mighty warrior who fought hard to defend his tribe in a time of chaos and change. It was the time before Israel was united under the kingship of Saul, David and Solomon. Charismatic leaders, "judges," arose who kept the people faithful to their covenant with God in the midst of a sea of idolatry. Gideon, Deborah, Samson all belong to this period.

Traditional interpretation of this story makes Samson the focus. The promised son Samson, would, due to the vow of his mother, be a Nazirite from birth and would free his people from their enemy (Judges 13). Interpreters point to John the Baptist's abstinence from wine (Luke 1:15) as well as Jesus' status as a Nazarene (Matthew 2:23) as being in the same tradition.

Be prepared for the story to lead you into a discussion of the merits of long hair and its connection with strength and identity. Many native male leaders today wear their hair in long braids. Hair style and length is one of the few remaining ways we can show our distinctiveness and uniqueness.

Our focus, however, is on Samson's unnamed mother. This wonderful story affirms the woman in two ways: by refusing to let her husband Manoah take over the script; and through her receiving of the visitation and commissioning of angels twice, thus emphasizing her spiritual sensitivity and independence. She immediately recognized the messengers as angels.

Her husband, though never doubting the message of the "messenger," thought the third angel was a "man." The words "angel" and "man" come from the same Hebrew word. Therefore the text is a play on words. Slowly, by observing that the "man" refused to eat, and gave his name in an obscure way (also a play on words) Manoah realized that this was not a man, but an angel. He then, however, drew inappropriate legalistic conclusions (Judges 13:22) and feared death, because he and his wife had seen God. His wife knows better.

She alone made the Nazirite vow on behalf of herself and her unborn child. Together they would fulfill its requirements. She was called to act in a way not dependent on her female anatomy, in order to support her son's calling. Her own participation in that vow played a significant role in helping deliver Israel from the Philistines.

She, not Manoah, pointed out the futility of showing miracles to people who had been singled out for death. She alone named the child. She, not Manoah, was confident of the future. And as spiritually mature as she is, she remains unnamed.

For Further Reading

Exum, Cheryl J. "Mother in Israel – A Familiar Figure Reconsidered." In *Feminist Interpretation of the Bible*, Letty Russell ed., Philadelphia: Westminster, 1985, pp. 82-85.

Fuchs, Esther. "The Literary Characterization of Mothers and Sexual Politics in the Hebrew Bible." Adela Yarboro Collins ed. In *Feminist Perspectives on Biblical Scholarship*, California: Scholars Press, 1985.

Laffey, Alice L. "Trust in God: Manoah's Unnamed Wife." In *An Introduction to the Old Testament*, Philadelphia: Fortress Press, 1988.

My Mother's Vow

My hair grows long
'Cause that's the vow
I'll free my people
But not right now.

Independent woman
Mother mine
The angel's promise
Was mighty fine.

My name is Samson. I am eight years old. My mother and my father Manoah are Israelites. For a long long time our enemies have been the Philistines.

"Mother," I asked her one day as she was kneading the bread dough. "I'm puzzled. Why is there some food you and me are forbidden to eat but father can have? And why don't you ever cut my hair? It's so long my friends threaten to use strands of it for a skipping rope."

She laughed out loud, shook the flour from her hands, and wiped them with a towel.

"Well son," she said, "at least they haven't braided your hair to make themselves a hammock to lie on."

She drew me on to her knee, put her arms around me and told me the story.

"For a long time I had no children. Then one day an angel came and told me that I was to have a baby. I was so surprised."

"What did the angel look like?" I asked.

"Short and fat, with a smiling face. The angel promised me that the baby would grow into a strong man. He would free our people from the Philistines."

I knew I was that baby. I jumped off her knee and gave a whoop. I pretended I was a soldier attacking the Philistines. She grinned at me. My father had joined us, but I still kept on with mother.

"But my hair, mother. My hair," I complained. "Why don't you cut it? Why don't you cut yours? My friends say we don't look after ourselves properly. They yell at me all the time. Even in my sleep.

'Hair, hair, what a snare.'"

I already knew the answer. But I wanted to hear it again.

"Well Samson, the angel said I must take the Nazirite vow for both of us: no wine, strong drink or unclean food were allowed us. You would be dedicated to God from your birth, and we were never to cut our hair. Hair is the secret of our strength. You know that."

I flexed my muscles as I thought strong men did, and grinned. I nodded my head in time to the beat of a song I made up,

"Hair so long, makes me strong,

Spare hair means I don't scare."

"So we're stuck with our long hair," I teased. "I won't cut mine until after I have defeated the Philistines," I bravely vowed. She nodded her head and smiled proudly.

Father had been sitting quietly all this time. I wondered if the angel had spoken to him as well.

"No, not a word," he said. "I prayed to God to send the messenger again, so we would know what to do."

"The angel's first visit was such a surprise," mother interrupted, "because it was a visit to me alone. Of course I ran to tell your father all about it."

"Did God answer your prayer, Father?" I asked.

"Yes, God's messenger did come again..." he began.

"... But only to me, when I was sitting by myself in the fields," my mother finished. "The second visit was another surprise. I ran as fast as I could and told your father."

"What happened next, Father?" I asked.

"Well," my father said, "we went to the fields and talked with the angel. The message was the same. The angel said that if you and your mother both kept the vow she had made, you would strike the first blow to free our people from the Philistines."

"But hadn't the angel told all that to Mother before?" I asked.

"Well yes," replied my father, "but I just wanted to make sure. I invited the stranger to a meal. He made some excuse, so I asked him his name."

"What was it?"

"Oh son," said my mother, "the strange being had no name as you have 'Samson.' The angel said, 'My name is wonderful.' That pointed us to God, whose works are full of wonder. It was an angel of God, not a man. Don't you see?"

I didn't see, but I didn't let on.

My father admitted that he certainly didn't see it right away. He'd never seen an angel before. Suddenly the messenger disappeared.

"We both fell on our faces," he continued.

I roared with laughter. I couldn't imagine my mother and father flat on their faces.

"It wasn't funny, son. I was afraid for our lives."

"But why would God let you see and hear the angel if you were about to die?"

"That's exactly what I said," my mother interrupted, her eyes sparkling with mischief.

"Your mother trusted God's promise more than I did, son," said my father.

She gave me an extra hug.

"When you were born, I myself named you Samson," she announced. "And I kept the vow, especially the part about not cutting your hair. So even if it gets so long it fills the whole kitchen, I'm not going to cut it."

"Even if it fills the whole house?"

"No."

"Even if it fills the whole world!"

"Definitely not."

"But all of the promise hasn't come true mother – that part

about me striking the first blow against the Philistines. I'm too young for that. I'm only eight years old."

"Yes you are. You will be the liberator of our people when you're older and stronger and wiser. That is a promise to me. And angels don't lie. But that's all ahead of you. Right now, it's time for bed."

I went off singing to myself,

"Hair so long it makes me strong.

Spare hair means I don't scare."

To find out if the angel's promise came true read Judges 14–16.

A Party to Remember
Mark 14:3–9

The story of the anointing of Jesus occurs at a critical juncture in his life. Jesus is on his way to Jerusalem for Passover but stops in Bethany. He is soon to die. His disciples are concerned only with success and glory. Jesus must have wondered if anyone understood his mission.

The story appears in Mark 14:3–9; Luke 7:36ff.; and John 12:1–8. Mark's gospel does not name the woman, and places the story at the home of Simon the Leper. The Markan version is the only one that has Mary anointing the head of Jesus, which in antiquity signified the instituting of a new king. To anoint the head was therefore a most daring and audacious action.

Luke, no longer understanding the story as one of a powerful woman prophet, replaces it with that of one who was "living an immoral life," and tells of the supper taking place at the home of Simon the Pharisee.

John identifies the woman as Mary of Bethany, in whose home the supper takes place. In this version it is Judas who misunderstands the woman's action. The bathing of another's feet was an act of hospitality and servanthood.

Only the story in Mark has the woman anoint Jesus' forehead, like the prophets anointing the kings of Israel. She alone understood his destiny as "king," his sharing of the suffering and pain of the poor, the women, the excluded. The disciples had misunderstood this point at least three times (Mark 14:31, Mark 9:32, Mark 10:32). They anticipated a kingdom of political power in which they hoped to share.

Against this quest for status women set their love and faithfulness. Lee Oo Chung writes of how the mothers in South Korea, whose sons were tortured because of their work with the poor, could no longer eat. The food choked them, so intimately did they identify with their sons. Only when Jesus' solidarity with the poor is recognized can we appreciate how subversive and prophetic Mary's action was. She implicitly recognized Jesus as the Messiah.

The phrase "the poor you have with you always" (Mark 14:7) has been used by some to assert that poverty can never be eradicated. It is still frequently used to convince the poor to accept their lot as the will of God. It is important that children clearly understand that poverty is not an unalterable God-given state of affairs. Indeed, Jesus rebukes Simon because he was not serious about the poor. The reference is to Deuteronomy 15:4–5: "There will never be any poor among you if only you obey the Lord your God by carefully keeping these commandments" (N.E.B.).

This audacious, intrusive act of the unknown prophetic woman, emphasizes that Jesus is on the side of the poor and that God's future belongs to them.

For Further Reading

Moltmann-Wendel, Elisabeth. *The Women Around Jesus*. London: SCM, 1982.

Wahlberg, Rachel Conrad. *Jesus According to a Woman*. New York: Paulist Press, 1975.

A Party to Remember

"There will not be poor among you"
The unknown woman knew,
"If you share their pain,
Break the poverty chain
And acts of justice do."

We had a big dinner party at our house last night. The dirty dishes piled high in the kitchen attest to that. My father Simon had invited some friends to a party. Jesus had brought Lazarus back to life. We wanted to celebrate.

The disciples James and Judas came. All the important men of the town came too. And, of course, Jesus was there. He was feeling sad because some men were angry with him and wanted to hurt him. We hoped the party would cheer him up.

The tables held great trays of food and jugs of refreshing drink. Fish. Olives. Bread. Cheese. It smelled so good!

Suddenly my father Simon put down his spoon with a clatter.

"What's that wonderful smell?" he asked, sniffing the air.

"It's not food," said James, one of Jesus' friends. "It smells more like perfume."

It was perfume all right. I'd seen a woman come in the back. She entered the room quietly. She carried a small bottle in her hand. With the other, she put her finger across her lips.

"Sh-sh-sh," she signaled to me.

She opened the bottle, poured some perfumed oil into her hand, and touched it to Jesus' head. Then she poured the rest on his head until the bottle was empty. He didn't say a word while all this was going on!

Then he turned to James. "You're right, James. It *is* perfume. See, this woman has given me a gift." He gestured to the woman who was now crouched down behind him, holding the empty bottle of perfume.

"What's a woman doing crashing our party?" sputtered James. "That woman touched Jesus. How dare she!" Judas cried.

"Anointing the head with perfumed oil is only for kings!" complained an important man from town.

The woman hung her head and looked at the floor. She didn't say a word. I could tell by her face that she wanted to cry.

"Why was the perfumed oil wasted in this way?" raged a rich man. "It cost a lot of money. It shouldn't have been wasted."

"You're right," said Judas. "It could have been sold for a lot of money and the money given to the poor."

I felt sorry for the woman. She had only meant to honor Jesus. Then Jesus smiled at the woman.

"Let her alone. Why do you make trouble for her?" he said.

The woman stood up. Her face had changed. A smile flickered across her face.

"She has done a beautiful thing for me," Jesus said. "You can help the poor whenever you like. They will still be here tomorrow because you do not keep the commandments, and you do not share with them."

Lazarus was quiet. I could almost hear James' stomach growl as it churned with anger. His face was so red it was fit to burst. My dad Simon was staring hard at his sandals.

"But I won't be with you much longer," Jesus said. "This woman knows that. She has done something special for me right now."

The woman's face glowed with joy. I wanted to whistle.

"Truly," said Jesus, "this woman whose name you don't even know has understood me. What she has done will be told everywhere in the whole world in memory of her."

The woman looked at Jesus. Her eyes seemed to say, "Thank you." Then she picked up the empty bottle and proudly left the room.

So much for my dad's all-male parties.

Joanna
Luke 8:3, 24:10

In the Greek scriptures, women gave strong consistent leadership to the emerging Christian community. However, their contributions were not given the same importance as those of the male disciples. This history needs to be recovered because it is women's history today – it is our story.

Women associated themselves with Jesus from the start. Jesus restored many women to health, community, and wholeness. He enabled them to give equal leadership with men in the community. To "be healed from evil spirits and infirmities" did not necessarily mean that the women were sick, or had been healed from physical diseases, or that they followed Jesus simply out of gratitude. Lee Oo Chung, a South Korean theologian, points out that the Greek word *therapuo*, which means to heal a disease, is *not* the word used in Luke 8:2. Rather, the Greek word *apoluo* is used, which means "to be set free," in these instances, from the types of bondage that inhibit women's full maturity.

Some of these women supported Jesus with "their substance." At the cross, when the male disciples fled, the women remained to mourn. They were the first to experience the Resurrection and to spread the good news, although they were not believed. As the early Christian community grew, women preached alongside men, went on missionary journeys, directed communities, taught the children, and hosted house churches. Yet much of this early history has not been highlighted in the Greek scriptures. As a result, it appears as though it was only men who gave major leadership. In her work with the gospels and the letters of Paul, Elisabeth Schussler Fiorenza finds evidence for an early Jesus movement that was thoroughly egalitarian and included powerful women.

Joanna was one of these women. An obscure figure, the wife of Herod's steward Chuza, she appears two or three times in the records. She supports Jesus "with her substance," mourns him on the cross, and is present with the other women at the empty tomb. She has a political background, being associated by marriage with Herod's corrupt and adulterous court.

We do not know if Joanna "left all" and followed Jesus as did the male disciples. If she did so, she would have caused a scandal in patriarchal society. The male disciples, on the other hand, were commended for their swift response to Jesus' call. We do know that she remained at the cross when the men had fled. She went to anoint the body of Jesus, while the male disciples hid in despair.

Her story is important because it illustrates one of the many women whose life was transformed from death to life through Jesus. In that sense her story is our story. It is important for children to know the stories of women like Joanna as well as the stories of Peter, James, and John, and the male disciples.

For Further Reading

Fiorenza, Elisabeth Schussler. "The Jesus Movement as Renewal Movement within Judaism." In *In Memory of Her*, New York: Crossroad, 1983, pp. 118–159.

Weems, Renita. "Certain Women." In *Just a Sister Away: A Womanist View of Women's Relationships in the Bible*, San Diego: Luramedia, 1988.

Joanna

You gotta choose Chuza
The palace said.
But I replied,
I'd rather be dead.

My name is Joanna. I used to live in a splendid palace. Most of the people at the palace called me "Chuza's wife," because they didn't know me.

They knew only my husband Chuza because he was an important man. He was King Herod's treasurer. There were many parties at the palace. There was always lots to eat: grapes, melons, figs, dates, and oranges. The best dancers in the country entertained Herod. The couches and chairs were made of solid gold, and decorated with jewels and precious stones. But the palace was not as splendid as it seemed. I didn't go to the parties because I knew Herod's palace was a wicked place.

"Where is Chuza's wife?" the servants would whisper. "Why isn't she here at his side?"

"Why is Chuza's wife not here at the banquet?" Herod's steward would ask.

Chuza's wife. Chuza's wife. Why didn't anyone call me Joanna? People only noticed me because I was married to Chuza. At first everything was exciting, but then it became deadly dull!

One day, I heard about Jesus from one of the children of a palace servant.

"He's passing through our town. Why don't we go and see him? You can meet my mother," said Rachel. "She's going to see him."

We gathered some flowers and walked as fast as we could to the place where Jesus was teaching. What a crowd there was! Everywhere we looked there were people – tall, small, fat, thin, happy, and serious people.

Rachel strained to see over their heads. At first we couldn't see Jesus at all.

We sat on the grass under a tree filled with twittering sparrows. They were playing hide-and-seek in the branches. The smaller ones were flying so fast they seemed to be in danger of falling to the ground. Our flowers began to wilt. At first Rachel couldn't see her mother Susanna anywhere. Finally she found her and we sat together.

We could hear Jesus' firm voice.

"If a sparrow falls, God knows it," Jesus was saying. "Every hair on your head is precious. Don't be afraid; you are worth more than hundreds of sparrows."

I was astonished. Nobody had ever told me I was precious.

We found a gap in the crowd and wiggled our way to the front. Then we saw him!

When Jesus finished speaking I gathered all my courage and went up to him.

"I am Chuza's wife," I said shyly.

"Don't you have a name?" Jesus asked.

I was so surprised I think my mouth fell open.

"My name is Jo-Jo-Joanna," I stammered.

"Peace be with you, Joanna," Jesus said.

I felt as though Jesus had colored me my favorite color— green. I felt as though I were part of a rainbow. I felt important, and not because I am Chuza's wife. I am precious because I am Joanna.

When I returned to the palace, I gathered up as much gold as I could carry. I wanted to help Jesus' work. I joined Susanna, and her friend Mary of Magdala, and other women. We joined the twelve disciples who went with Jesus as he preached in the towns and villages. Now I was called Joanna. Now I knew I was precious. I felt alive again.

Women Committed to Justice
(Then and Now)

Why Not? (Five Sisters)
Numbers 27, 28

This story is one that women in Latin America deem very important since it is "their" story too. The struggle of Christians there revolves around land, justice, and the sharing of resources. Too often the women have been left out of that story. Here is a story in which they are central.

The focus of this story is on the ability and persistence of five women who got the land inheritance laws changed, not only for themselves, but for all Israel.

This is the story of five ancient feminists, five original thinkers, and five social innovators. They propose to the community an innovative inheritance policy. They directly attack the male-centred economic system and social thought. (Samuel Rayan, s.j., in In Christ: Power of Women, 1986.)

To understand the essence of this story one must first understand the practice of Levirate marriage.

A Levirate marriage was the marriage of a widow to the brother of her dead husband. It was designed to preserve the property of a man for his male descendants, and to protect and give security to the widow. (Phyllis Bird, "Images of Women in the Old Testament," in Religion and Sexism.)

Poverty is the problem in Latin America. Our poor are those whose main task it is to survive. Women and children are most affected by poverty. Poverty is a challenge for women, who must either accept everything as it is, or fight for life. The woman who claims a better life does not claim it against men. She does it to get better conditions of human existence, and from there she questions her relationship to others. Poverty has to do with exploitation. That is why it is linked to patriarchy. (Rachel Rodrigues, "Hope against Hope," in Speaking for Ourselves, 1990.)

Women in Israel were prohibited from inheriting property for a sound reason. Basic inheritance laws concerning daughters guarded against the alienation and loss of family property. Since a daughter usually left her father's house at marriage and became a member of her husband's family, she normally received no inheritance. Neither did the wife since property was transmitted through the male line.

Two special laws later developed. Daughters were permitted to inherit where there were no sons, as in our story (Numbers 27). But they were only place holders in the male line, which was thereby enabled to continue through their children. The law was further modified in the interests of tribal solidarity and preservation of the tribal land by a specification that the daughter who had inherited marry within her father's tribe (Numbers 36). So it is clear that it is the daughter's husband who is the real heir. Women were the blood links to pass property from male to male within the family line. Women had very little chance of owning property, although the management of land was frequently undertaken by women.

For Further Reading

Bird, Phyllis. "Images of Women in the Old Testament." In *Religion and Sexism*, Rosemary R. Ruether ed., New York: Simon and Schuster, 1974.

Laffey, Alice J. "Zelophehad's Docile Daughters." In *An Introduction to the Old Testament—A Feminist Perspective*, Philadelphia: Fortress Press, 1988, p. 58.

Rayan, Samuel. *In Christ: Power of Women*. Stree Reflect Series 4, All India Council of Christian Women (Sub-unit of the National Council of Churches in India) Madras, 1986.

Rodrigues, Rachel. "Hope against Hope." In *Speaking for Ourselves*, Wendy Robins and Musimbi R. A. Kanyoro. eds., Geneva: WCC, 1990.

Sakenfeld, Katharine Doob. "Feminist Biblical Interpretation." In *Theology Today*, July 1989.

Why Not? (Five Sisters)

story by Jean Little, Guelph, Ontario

In a long ago time and a far away land, there lived a man who had five daughters and no sons. His friends felt sorry for him.

"It is sad for you, Zelophehad," they said, "that your wife died before giving you a man child. It must grieve you to have no son to follow after you."

"I have five fine girls," Zelophehad told them. "Mahlah and Noah and Hoglah and Milcah and little Tirzah. What need have I of a boy?"

His friends shook their heads at this.

"When we come to the land Yahweh has promised us," they said, "we will each have property of our own. Then we and our sons will plant wheat and grow vines and pasture sheep and pull fish from the rills and prosper. But you will have to work alone. Hired help is not like family. If only you had a son!"

Zelophehad laughed.

"You don't know my daughters," he said. "They will all help me.

"Mahlah will sow the seeds
and pull the weeds
and harvest the fields
and bring the yield
to the threshing floor
and put the grain in barns to store.

"Mahlah and I spend hours discussing what crops we'll raise.

"Noah will plant the vines
where the sunlight shines
and choose the fruit
for making wine.
'It will be good and sweet,' she says.

"Noah and I talk daily about our vineyard on its warm slope.

"Hoglah wants to be my shepherd. She'll mate the ewes
with sturdy rams
and help to birth
the tiny lambs
and lead her flock to pastures green
and keep them safe from harms unseen.

"Hoglah and I talk for hours about caring for our flocks.

"Milcah can pull the fish from the rills
and snare the conies in the hills
She fills our pot
with savory stew
There's nothing at all
my daughters can't do."

Zelophehad's friends looked at the girls and snorted. But they tried to be polite.

"Four of your daughters sound fine," they said at last, "but what about little Tirzah? She is so small and shy. She can't help to plant your fields or tend your vines or guard your sheep or fish your rills."

Zelophehad smiled down at his youngest child who was trying to hide behind him.

"My Tirzah may seem small and shy to you," he said fondly, "but she sings and tells stories and makes jokes. Without her, this long desert journey would have been endless. Tirzah can make us laugh. She is also the one who thinks most clearly. Someday my little Tirzah will surprise you all. Wait and see."

Zelophehad and his daughters went on traveling with Moses through the wilderness toward the promised land. When they sat by their fire in the evening, he and his five growing girls dreamed of what they would do when they had their own land. Over and over they said the same words.

"I'll sow the seeds and pull the weeds," said Mahlah.

"I'll tend the vines and make the wine," said Noah.

"Over the sheep good watch I'll keep," said Hoglah.

"I'll fish the rills and hunt the hills," said Milcah.

When Tirzah did not say a word, they teased her gently. "What will little Tirzah do?" they asked.

Tirzah just smiled. She could see that there would be plenty of work left for her to do. But she didn't say so.

When they drew near to the promised land and the five little girls had become young women, Zelophehad died. His four older daughters wailed and moaned, mourning for him.

"Our dear father is gone," wept Mahlah, "and we will never have the land he was promised. I will never sow the seeds and pull the weeds for him."

"Our dear father is gone," sobbed Noah, "and I will never plant the vines and make the wines with him."

"Our dear father is dead," grieved Hoglah, "and now I will never walk with him beside our flock."

"Our dear father is dead," whimpered Milcah, "and now I will never fish the rills and hunt the hills for him."

"Why not?" said Tirzah.

The others stopped crying and stared at her.

"Did you say something, Tirzah?" asked Mahlah and Noah and Hoglah and Milcah.

"Yes," said Tirzah. "I know our father is gone, and I too grieve for him. But why won't you plant and tend and herd and hunt in the land Moses promised our father?"

The other girls stared at her as though she had gone mad.

"Because we aren't boys," they said. "Girls can't plant and tend and herd and fish without their father. Moses and Eleazar and the priests and the people would never let us."

"Why not?" asked Tirzah.

"Tirzah, don't be stupid. You know that daughters never inherit land, only sons," the older girls snapped.

"Why not?" insisted Tirzah. "Father said we could. 'There's nothing at all my girls can't do.' Remember? Let's at least ask."

"It wouldn't work," said Milcah.

"It's no use," said Hoglah.

"They'd never listen," sighed Noah.

"Not to girls," Milcah added mournfully.

"Cowards!" jeered little Tirzah. "I never thought you were so spineless. What would Father say if he could hear you?"

"He'd be ashamed," said Mahlah after a second's silence.

"He believed we could do anything," said Noah.

"Maybe Tirzah is right," said Hoglah slowly.

"Let's try," said Milcah. "It can't hurt to try."

"Stand tall," Tirzah instructed her four tall sisters. "Look them right in the eye. Remember Father's faith in us. Let Mahlah do the talking."

"And what will you do?" Noah asked with a laugh.

"I will pray to Yahweh," said Tirzah.

So Zelophehad's five daughters went to Moses and Eleazar and the priests and the people. Mahlah did the talking. Hoglah and Noah and Milcah stood right behind her to back her up. Tirzah waited in the shadows.

"We are the daughters of Zelophehad. Is it right that just because our father had no sons his name should disappear from the tribe and the land be lost? Let us inherit our father's portion of land," Mahlah said.

"I, Mahlah, will sow the seeds and pull the weeds,

Noah, will tend the vines and make the wine,

Milcah will fish the rills and hunt the hills,

And over the sheep good watch Hoglah will keep.

We planned it all with Father. He taught us everything he knew. We know just what to do."

"Didn't your father have one more daughter?" Moses asked.

"Yes," said the others. "She is here with us but she is very shy. Her name is Tirzah. She will help however she can."

Moses went into the Holiest of Holy Places to talk to Yahweh. But Tirzah, standing outside with the rest, had talked to Yahweh first. This is what she had said.

"Mahlah will sow the seeds and pull the weeds,

Noah will tend the vines and make the wine,

Milcah will fish the rills and hunt the hills,

And over the sheep good watch Hoglah will keep.

"I, Tirzah, will cook fine meals from Mahlah's fields.

I will serve the wine from Noah's vines.

I will cut and fillet all of Milcah's prey.

I will weave good cloth from the wool of Hoglah's flocks."

Yahweh smiled at little Tirzah just as her father had always done.

When Moses was silent, the Lord God spoke.

"Let the law of the Israelites be changed. Let the daughters of Zelophehad inherit their father's portion," God said. "They are good girls and they deserve their chance."

So Mahlah and Noah and Hoglah and Milcah and little Tirzah had their chance and they did well. Their crops grew green and bore much grain. Their wine grew famous. Their fleeces were the whitest and softest of all. And neighbors kept dropping by to share their fish dinners.

The young men of their clan got worried. They went to Moses and Eleazar and the priests.

"What if the daughters of Zelophehad marry foreigners?" they asked. "Then the land they have made so plentiful will go to strangers. They should have to marry men of their own clan. They should have to marry us."

Moses spoke to Yahweh about this and Yahweh smiled again. There were 50,000 men in the clan. And Yahweh knew well that Zelophehad's daughters had already set their hearts on five of them.

"They shall marry into the clan," said Yahweh, "but they may marry whomever they please."

Moses and the priests and the people came and told the five daughters of Zelophehad that they must marry men of their own clan. Mahlah and Noah and Hoglah and Milcah looked at each other and tossed their heads.

"We don't need husbands," said Mahlah. "I can plant the seeds and pull the weeds myself."

"We don't need husbands," sniffed Noah. "I can tend the vines and make the wine alone."

"We don't need husbands," scoffed Hoglah. "Over my sheep good watch I keep."

"We don't need husbands," Milcah said proudly. "I hunt the

hills and fish the rills better by myself."

Then Tirzah smiled into her sisters' angry faces and spoke to them softly.

"We do need husbands," she said, her eyes sparkling with laughter, "because without husbands, we will have no daughters to follow after us. Don't you want daughters?"

The others stopped scowling and started smiling ever so slightly.

"Yes, Tirzah, you are right," said Mahlah and Hoglah and Noah and Milcah. "We want daughters. But we want to choose our husbands ourselves."

"May we choose our own husbands?" Tirzah asked Moses and Eleazar and the priest and the assembled people.

Moses looked unhappy but he said, "You may choose. Yahweh has said it."

"Well then, why not?" said Tirzah.

The Widow Who Kept On
Luke 18:1–5

Luke wrote this story sometime around 90 to 110 CE, some 50 years after the life of Jesus. Luke records the story as a parable told by Jesus.

What is the main point of the story? Luke prefaces the story by saying that "He spoke to them a parable to show they should keep on praying and never lose heart."

But as Rachel Conrad Wahlberg suggests in her book *Jesus and the Freed Woman*, Jesus himself does not present the story as a model for prayer as Luke does. It doesn't fit. Surely Jesus would not offer us a God unconcerned with justice (as the judge is portrayed), who gives in only because he gets tired of a woman pestering him! Rather, if justice is granted on a human level (given persistence), then why doubt that God will grant justice? Surely God will listen to us more readily than the unjust judge.

Just as the early Christians did not immediately rise up against slavery, neither did they rise up to defend widows as strongly as they should have. That is why there are so many biblical injunctions on behalf of widows. The prophets Isaiah and Jeremiah defended widows, and emphasized the obligations that supported them.

"Pursue justice and champion the oppressed,

Give the orphan rights, plead the widow's cause" (Isaiah 1:17).

"Do not oppress the alien, the orphan, the widow" (Jeremiah 7:6).

Old Testament scholar Phyllis Bird writes that women were dependent on support from their father before marriage, and from their husband, and then sons, after marriage. The plight of a widow without sons was desperate. Her dead husband's property would pass to the nearest male relative, who was under no obligation to maintain the widow. She would be expected to return to her own family (usually an impossible option) or to enter into a levirate marriage. This meant her husband's brother would marry her and support her.

The action of the widow is the emphasis in this story. Jesus affirms a widow who demonstrates courage, persistence, and the determination not to give up in the face of enormous obstacles, especially in the public domain.

It may help to read this story together with "The Chipko Women," a factual story from India, and "The Long Struggle for Justice," a story from South Korea. Closer to home, you may want to read "The Courage to Be," Peggy Monague's story about her struggle as a native person in Canada.

For Further Reading

Bird, Phyllis. "Images of Women in the Old Testament." In *Religion and Sexism*, Rosemary Radford Ruether, ed., New York: Simon and Schuster, 1974.

Wahlberg, Rachel Conrad. *Jesus and the Freed Woman*. New York: Paulist Press, 1978.

The Widow Who Kept On

The widow fearless
Of the unjust judge,
Demanded justice,
And made him budge.

Knock Knock!
"Put on the lights,"
That widow again,
Comes for her rights.

In a certain city there lived a judge. He didn't care about people. He didn't care about animals. He didn't care about God. He cared only about himself.

In that same city there lived a widow. She lived alone. Because she didn't have enough money to feed herself, she agreed to sell her house. But the man who bought her house then told her he would pay her only half the amount they had agreed on.

The widow knew she was being cheated. She knew her rights. She also knew nobody would listen to her. She had no one who would speak for her to the judge. So she went herself.

"I will ask for justice for myself," she said.

One night she went to the judge's house.

Knock, knock.

Put on the lights,

Here comes that widow,

Wanting her rights.

"I want justice."

The judge thought to himself, "Why should I be bothered with this widow's complaint? She is a nobody. Why should I listen to her?" So he dismissed her case and sent her away.

That same night she prayed to God.

"Friend of all the weak, suckle me and feed me, that I may be strong."

She woke up early the next morning. She was angry. She thought about being cheated out of her money. She decided to go back to the judge and ask again for the full payment for her house.

Knock, knock.

Put on the lights,

That widow again

Comes for her rights.

"I want justice."

The judge said to himself, "She's back again. She acts as if she is somebody. She wants justice. But she's only a poor widow."

Again he refused to help her. He told the widow that people would not like her if she kept on pestering him. He certainly would not like her.

The widow didn't care if people didn't like her. She didn't care if the judge didn't like her. She cared about justice. So she went back a third time.

Knock, knock.
Put on the lights
That widow again
Comes for her rights.
"I want justice."

This time the judge was very upset. He wondered if she intended to come to him every day for the next year until justice was done. How tiresome! He said to himself "She is such a nuisance. I will see she gets justice before she wears me out."

To get rid of her, the judge made the man who had cheated the widow pay her what he owed her. The widow was glad she had stood up for herself.

Knock, knock.
I have my rights,
Others will soon,
With them I'll fight!

The Chipko Women

This story is a contemporary parallel to Jesus' parable of the widow and the unjust judge, found in Luke 18:1–5. The same themes are emphasized: poor women, powerlessness against injustice, the "rightness" of the women's cause, dogged persistence until justice is finally done.

The struggle of the Chipko women took place between 1973 and 1982 in Advani, a small village in the foothills of the Himalayas in the Tehri Garwahl district in India. For nine years, tribal women protested the cutting of the trees and the implicit loss of their resources. In Hindi, *chipko* means "the women who hug."

The source from which I have adapted this story is "Women in Praise and Struggle" in the ISPCK (International Society for Promoting Christian Knowledge), Delhi, 1982, edited by Jyotsna Chatterji.

The Chipko Women

Chip, chop, chip, chop,
We finally got the axes to stop,
Chip, chop, chip, chop,
Destroying trees was quite a flop.

Vimala stamped her foot and muttered to herself. Two small children blocked her way on the narrow pathway.

All day she had been collecting wood to cook the evening meal. Now she would be late because the two girls were so slow. She peered out from under the heavy bundle of branches on her bent-over back, shook her fist, and called out, "Hurry up now. Hurry up."

The two girls could go no faster. They too were bent over with the load of twigs and branches on their backs. Every day they climbed the steep hill from the village to the forest to collect wood so that their families could cook the evening meal.

Lakshmi, the oldest, was nine years old. She had been climbing this same pathway since she was four years old.

Just as the path opened out into a clearing, Vimala's husband came running to meet her. He had important news to tell. Men with axes were going to cut down the pine trees in the morning. A big company wanted wood for skateboards. It was against the law to cut the trees. The forest had been there for the villagers for years and years. The mayor had been paid a lot of money to let the company cut the trees.

Vimala thought and thought. She had collected branches and twigs from that forest all her life.

"If the trees are cut, where will I get fuel to cook supper? The forest gives fuel."

She ran to her neighbor.

"If the trees are cut, where will we get fertilizer for the crops? The forest gives fertilizer."

They ran to another neighbor.

"If the trees are cut, where will we get the rich soil that makes our gardens grow good food? The forest gives food."

They ran to another neighbor.

"If the trees are cut, where will we get bark and roots to weave sturdy mats to cover our floors? The forest gives fiber."

They ran to another neighbor.

"If the trees are cut, where will we get straw and hay to feed the cows? The forest gives fodder."

In no time at all, 50 women knew about the plot to cut the trees down in the morning. They knew the forest would no longer be there to give them fuel, fertilizer, food, fodder, and fiber.

Vimala and the others didn't know what to do. They were poor. They had no money. They couldn't read or write. Nobody would listen to them.

They were sad. They knew it was wrong to cut the trees that had helped the villagers for so many years. They didn't have anything to help them fight for the forest they loved so much. They sat together and talked.

Finally Vimala said, "We do have our bodies. Let's use them." The others had no idea what she meant.

The next morning at dawn, 50 women slowly climbed up the path to the forest. Each woman chose a tree, put her arms around its trunk, and hugged it. When the axemen came to cut the trees, the women wouldn't budge. All day the axemen tried to persuade them to stop hugging the trees. Not one woman moved. At nightfall, the axemen left the forest.

Three years later, greedy men who wanted the wood to build factories hired axemen to return to the forest.

Lakshmi was now 12 years old. She had learned in school that if all the trees in one place were cut down, the soil would be washed away by the great swollen rivers that flooded down the hills. She told Vimala. Again Vimala called all the women together. The next morning, at dawn, 50 women slowly climbed up the path to the pine forest. Each woman chose a splendid tree and hugged it. They held on tightly even when the axemen came and tried to get them to stop hugging the trees.

Lakshmi had learned to print. She had made a big banner. She colored the "F" brilliant green, and all the other letters, colors of the rainbow: yellow, orange, red, blue, indigo, and violet. She hung it between the two biggest trees. The banner said,

Trees give the 5 "F's"
Fuel, Fertilizer, Food, Fiber, and Fodder

The axemen didn't like her sign, but they didn't cut down the trees. After an hour or so, 100 police came and arrested the women. They put them in jail for two weeks. But 50 other village women came at dawn every day and hugged the trees. The axemen finally went away.

Six years later, the same thing happened again. This time, 500 women came to the forest at dawn. They had become famous. They were known as "the Chipko women," which, in their language, means "the women who hug." And the axemen never again came to cut the trees.

The Long Struggle for Justice

Here is another contemporary story of powerless women and the unjust judge. I have adapted this story from material from *From the Womb of Han – Stories of Korean Women Workers,* published by the Christian Conference of Asia, Hong Kong, 1982. The Buddhist Korean poet Ko Eun writes, "We Koreans were born from the womb of Han and brought up in the womb of Han. Han is a deep feeling of indignation about injustice and a yearning *for* justice."

In the Korean workplace, women are always subordinate to their male counterparts. Their wages are one half of those of male workers. They have long hours and are victims of verbal abuse. Because they come from poor families, they usually tolerate all this to keep their jobs. The story of the Hai Tai workers comes out of the history of the women workers movement in Korea, which has become a focal point of the movement for democracy in that country.

Some of the women in the story belong to the "minjung" or "people's" church. Its members are workers from the factories. It tries to give support to alienated workers. Its purpose is not to increase its membership but to nurture a liberated community, and to resist unjust authorities. If the membership grows, that is good too.

The Long Struggle for Justice

Kang-ja was 11 years old. She had two black pigtails tied with bright red ribbons. She didn't go to school. She had to work hard, in order to earn money for her parents, who were very poor. She packed biscuits at the Hai Tai Biscuit Factory from dawn until dark.

She worked 12 hours every day and 18 hours on Sunday. Most days she was so-o-o tired.

Every day she trudged three kilometres to the factory. On her way she passed the Buddhist temple and heard its gong.

"Bong, bong," it sounded.

Its deep notes made her feel sorry for herself. She passed the small boys working in the sunny rice fields. She wished she could work alongside them instead of going to the dark factory.

Kang-ja was tired. S-o-o-o tired!

She was tired of the long walk to work. She was tired of working long hours. She was tired of eating only oranges, eggs, and biscuits for lunch.

"I wish I could eat chicken, crab, and octopus," she said to herself. But her family was too poor to buy those things.

One day Kang-ja fell sick at the factory. A friend brought her home in her car.

"You rest now. You were so tired that you fainted," said the friend. To Kang-ja's parents the friend explained, "The boss didn't want anyone to know how he had overworked her. He covered her up with a newspaper and just left her in the corner. I found her. Take her to the hospital where she can have a good rest."

Kang-ja was in the hospital for 10 days. Then she came home. Her mother was glad to have her at home. But she was also worried. She knew that when Kang-ja went back to work, she might join the women and the other children who were complaining.

"It is against the law to have to work such long hours every day," they were telling the boss. "It's too much to work from breakfast until long past dinner at night."

Kang-ja knew that if she complained the boss wouldn't like her. Maybe she would lose her job. There would be fewer oranges, eggs, or biscuits on the table.

"There would never be any chicken, crab, or octopus for me to eat," she thought to herself. It was already so bad that Kang-ja's mother filled up on ginseng tea.

Kang-ja knew the boss was unfair. "He is wrong," she thought to herself. "Maybe there are more important things than what one eats. I would rather him treat me fairly than have chicken on our table." Finally she said it out loud.

"The boss treats us unfairly," she told her parents even though she was afraid.

"You are right, little daughter," said her mother and father. "Do what you must to get justice, even though it will be hard for all of us."

When Kang-ja returned to work, she found 50 women and children who were complaining about working such long hours. They were so-o-o tired. Soon there were 100 women and children complaining.

One day, they all decided to act. Kang-ja joined them. They worked for eight hours only, from breakfast to dinner. Then they went home. No more working after dinner for them.

When Kang-ja walked past the Buddhist temple on her way home, she again heard its gong.

"Bong, bong." The deep notes now seemed to give her hope. The sound made her walk seem shorter.

She did this for five days in a row.

The boss was very angry. On the fifth day, he locked the doors of the factory and tried to keep the women and children workers from going home. Kang-ja and her friends climbed out the windows!

Plop. Plop. It was a long fall to the ground.

Then the boss phoned the parents of Kang-ja and all the other children. He asked them to stop their daughters from making trouble. But the parents agreed with the children. Enough was enough. The boss was wrong.

Kang-ja knew she might lose her job. There might be fewer oranges, eggs, or biscuits on the table. She certainly couldn't buy chicken.

Some of Kang-ja's friends at the church told their friends how the law was being broken at the biscuit factory.

They walked in protest marches through the city streets.

They spoke at the church.

They kept bothering the boss.

He got so-o-o tired of them. He decided it would be easier to give them what they wanted. Maybe then they would stop complaining.

Finally, he agreed that they would work only eight hours every weekday. They would work only from breakfast to dinner. And he would pay them more money.

Kang-ja's mother would now have something besides ginseng tea. She would have chicken, crab, and octopus to eat.

Kang-ja continued to pass the Buddhist temple every day. The gong rang out with its hopeful "Bong, bong." The small boys in the rice fields looked up and waved cheerily at her.

She waved back, skipping joyously under the sunny skies.

The Courage to Be

This story, like the preceding ones, is about persistence and self-confidence in the face of injustice. It is adapted from an incident in the life of Peggy Monague, a Canadian aboriginal person.

The Courage to Be

adapted from the story of Peggy Monague,
Christian Island, Ontario

When I was a child, I was loved by my family and neighbors. I had lots of fun playing games in Rama, Ontario, where I was born. When I got to Grade Three, I had to take a bus to school every day to a nearby town called Orillia.

One day at school, a boy pushed me. I couldn't help spilling my books on the ground.

"Please pick them up," I asked.

"No," he spit back at me.

"Pick them up," I insisted, in a louder voice.

"Not going to, squaw," he shouted. "Indian squaw."

I was mad.

"You pick up my books. You made me drop them," I sputtered.

"Try and make me, squaw," he taunted. "You're nothing but an Indian squaw."

"Sticks and stones can break my bones but names can never hurt me," I shouted back.

The racket attracted the teacher's attention. She gave both of us a scolding. The boy never told me he was sorry. I was angry. He had done something to me that was not right.

I felt lonely, mad, proud, and stubborn all at the same time. I went home and told by mother. She told me to stand tall and believe in myself. She taught me that God is with us always, and not to fear anything or anybody.

Deep down inside I know I am an aboriginal person, not an Indian squaw. That boy was wrong. And now I know I will always be able to stand up for myself and what is right.

Women as Victims

Much of women's reality, both past and present, has been one of victimization at the hands of individuals, cultural systems, or patriarchal institutions. The following stories illustrate a small part of this history.

Leah
Genesis 29–30

Leah and Rachel were the two daughters of Laban. At the time of the biblical story, women's only security was in a marriage that their father would arrange. Men treated them as extremely valuable commodities, but commodities nevertheless.

Jacob worked for his uncle Laban and wished to receive as his wages Laban's daughter Rachel as his bride. It was rather like pre-paying for a bride. Rachel was more beautiful than her sister Leah, but because she was younger, was not entitled to marriage ahead of her older sister Leah.

Laban therefore deceived Jacob and gave him Leah. Because Jacob still desired Rachel, he worked another seven years for Laban in the hope of having Rachel. It was rather like paying off a mortgage.

Leah was not loved by her father Laban, or her sister Rachel, or her husband Jacob. Laban tricked Jacob into marrying her, because he knew he would have trouble finding her a husband. The text indicates that Leah had something wrong with her eyes. Various translations say, "dull-eyed, no sparkle, or weak," (Genesis 29:17). These terms seem to suggest that Leah was visually impaired. She was not a "catch" for Jacob.

How might she have felt when her father Laban palmed her off on Jacob? How does a woman who is visually impaired feel about someone arranging a man for her? How does anyone feel about being patronized by those of us who consider ourselves to be free of handicaps?

Leah responds with anger. We tell the story here to reinforce the idea that in cases of injustice or prejudice it is quite all right for the victim to feel angry.

For Further Reading

Exum, Cheryl J. "Mother in Israel—A Familiar Figure Reconsidered." In *Feminist Interpretation of the Bible*, Letty Russell ed., Philadelphia: Westminster Press, 1985, p. 79ff.

Jeansoone, Sharon Pace. *The Women of Genesis*. Minneapolis: Fortress, 1990.

Leah

Some have clear eyes, a beautiful face,
To have poor eyes is no disgrace,
Profoundly deaf or terribly lame,
It doesn't matter, they're not to blame.

"What a pity she isn't pretty. What's the matter with her eyes?"

Ever since I can remember, people have said that about me. It got worse when my little sister Rachel was born. Right in front of me people would say, "She's so much prettier than her sister Leah." Why did they pay so much attention to a baby? I was so mad I pulled out all the potted plants.

I knew there was something wrong with my eyes. When I was older I heard the other girls whisper and giggle whenever I walked by. They never let me join in. And I watched as they looked coyly at the boys in camp. They would whisper and then run off laughing. The other kids talked about the colors of the leaves and the beauty of the flowers, but to me those things were just a blur. I could see the trees and the sand dunes and the tents, but nothing smaller. So I squinted and frowned. Maybe if my eyes had been better people might have thought me beautiful.

When I grew up, Jacob came to work for my father, Laban. Rachel and I talked about it one evening.

"I was so excited," she whispered to me. "I met him at the well. He was so strong that he rolled the stone off the mouth of the well so I could get water for the sheep. And handsome too! His name is Jacob."

"Did he like you," I whispered back.

"He liked me all right. He kissed me, Leah. Imagine!" She giggled. "All the herdsmen saw it. He told me I was beautiful, and his eyes filled with tears."

I wished I had been at the well instead of Rachel. But Jacob probably wouldn't have kissed me. Nobody's eyes ever filled with tears when they looked at me.

"I hope Father lets him stay with us," Rachel said. "Can you imagine having him around here all the time?"

I tried, but even in my imagination Jacob chose Rachel.

Father did allow Jacob to stay with us. And every morning when Jacob went to the fields, Rachel waved goodbye to him and blew him kisses. She's such a flirt.

Jacob had worked for our father for a month, before father asked, "Are you going to continue working for me without getting paid? Tell me what wages you want."

Jacob said, "I want Rachel. I will work without wages for seven years if you promise to give her to me." Father agreed.

It wasn't fair. I was the eldest daughter. It was not right to promise the marriage of Rachel before mine was arranged. But I didn't say anything to Rachel because Jacob had fallen in love with her. No wonder. Everyone said she was so graceful and beautiful. I was jealous of her for that. Why couldn't I have been born with clear eyes and a beautiful face?

Seven years passed and again Jacob said, "I want Rachel."

Father made a big feast and killed the fatted calf. Just after sunset, when it was getting so dark I couldn't see my hand in front of my face, he told me to follow him into a nearby tent. He told me Jacob would be sharing the tent with me that night. I was not to say anything, but just do as I was told. I had no choice. I was only his daughter.

Shortly after Father left, Jacob came into the tent. Jacob had no idea it was me, not Rachel. He wanted Rachel. He did not want me. I couldn't believe Father had done this to me. I may have wanted Jacob too, but not like this! Did Father think it would be so difficult to find me a husband that he had to trick Jacob? I felt crushed and ashamed.

When morning came, Jacob saw that it was me and not Rachel. He flung himself out of the tent and stormed over to Laban.

"Why have you done this to me?" he exploded. "Did I not work seven years for Rachel? I want her, not her dull-eyed sister."

My head ached.

"It is not right to give Rachel the younger sister in marriage before Leah, the elder. Join the seven-day feast for Leah, and I shall give you Rachel if you work for me for another seven years."

I felt sick to my stomach.

Jacob joined in the seven-day feast in my honor but he never looked at me the whole time.

Was I so ugly? It wasn't my fault there was something wrong with my eyes. Jacob didn't even treat me kindly. Was it because I had to squint and frown because of my eyesight? Was it because that meant I didn't have a beautiful face?

I was so mad I wanted to go outside and kick a camel.

———

Hagar
Genesis 16, 21

Generally, when church people speak of women in the Bible, they choose to highlight famous women like Sarah... They never mention women slaves who were pagan, such as Hagar. (Elsa Tamez, "The Woman Who Complicated the History of Salvation," in New Eyes for Reading, *1986.)*

Hagar was a woman oppressed four times over: she was a slave, a woman, a foreigner, and a woman of color. She was rejected three times (Genesis 16:1–2, 4–14, 21:8–21) by both Sarah and Abraham. She suffered and had no advocate. Today, third world women claim this as their story. It reveals to the oppressed of the earth the story of God's salvation.

Theologian Esther Fuchs suggests that the conflict in the story is not simply between mistress and handmaiden as the text suggests. It was about the pain experienced by women caught in patriarchal institutions that offered so few options, in this instance **both** Sarah and Hagar. Neither of them had much room to maneuver. An impossible situation eventually pitted them against each other.

For Further Reading

Tamez, Elsa. "The Woman Who Complicated the History of Salvation." In *New Eyes for Reading,* by John Pobee and Barbel von Wartenber-Potter, WCC, 1986.

Fuchs, Esther. "The Literary Characterization of Mothers and Sexual Politics in the Hebrew Bible." In *Feminist Perspectives on Biblical Scholarship,* Adela Yaboro Collins ed , California Scholars Press, 1985.

The One Who Sees Me (Hagar)
Genesis 16

Sarah is barren. She decides to give her maidservant Hagar to Abraham so that she can claim as her own the children born of that union. This solution was not a bold new initiative on Sarah's part. It was acceptable legal practice within the Near Eastern world.

Hagar conceives and becomes quite chippy towards Sarah. When Sarah receives permission from Abraham to reassert control over her slave, she abuses Hagar. Hagar responds by running away, setting out through the desert for her home in Egypt.

Her escape is stopped by an angel of God, who commands her to return to Sarah. The angel promises that Hagar's offspring too will be innumerable. Hagar returns and bears a son, whom she calls Ishmael.

In this story as traditionally told, God's concern is for the male child that will be born, and the great nation he will foster because he is Abraham's son – a thoroughly patriarchal viewpoint.

Our story will focus on Hagar. She is the only *woman* in the Hebrew scriptures who has had the privilege of seeing and talking with God (Chapter 16).

But Hagar is an Egyptian slave woman. How was it that she had this privilege?

Elsa Tamez states, "The oppressed are also God's children, co-creators of history. God does not leave them to perish in the desert without leaving a trace. They must live to be part of history, and struggle to be subjects of it."

The God who orders her to return to her oppressive mistress in this first story seems not to resemble the God of the Exodus and the Red Sea crossing. Yet it is Hagar's only hope for a future. She becomes a co-creator of history by making her own decisions in the light of her vision of God. Her flight and her readiness to risk everything in the wilderness signal her openness to the future.

The One Who Sees Me (Hagar)

A woman who is dark,
So poor and a slave,
That's who God
Decides to save.

Dark and foreign,
In pain, and poor,
That's who God loves,
And that's for sure!

Hagar was a poor young slave girl from Egypt.

Sarah, her mistress, was a Hebrew. Sarah was too old to have a baby. She was very beautiful. But she was unhappy. God had promised to make her husband, Abraham, father of "a great nation." His descendants were to be as numerous as the stars in the sky. But how could this be if she couldn't have children. She had to find some way of providing Abraham with a son.

Then Sarah had an idea. Maybe Hagar her slave could have a baby for Abraham. In those days, slaves often had to do this. Then Sarah would claim the baby as her own. She would feel important and Abraham would have his son. It didn't matter how Hagar felt, she was only a slave.

But it didn't work that way. Hagar was going to have a baby all right. But instead of making Sarah happy it made her mad. Sarah really wanted to have the baby herself. To make things worse, Hagar started to boast to Sarah. Hagar even made up a little song.

"Sarah can't have one
'Cause she's too old,
I'm going to have one
And it makes me bold."

Hagar told the other slaves how she was going to have a baby and Sarah wasn't. She thought Abraham would think her more important than Sarah.

Sarah heard Hagar bragging. She went to Abraham.

"The foreign slave girl Hagar is saying rude things about me to the other slaves. She thinks she's better than I am just because she's going to have a baby. What are you going to do about her?"

"She's your problem," said Abraham. "Do with her as you like." Abraham didn't really care what happened to Hagar, as long as he had a son.

So Sarah tried to make Hagar's life difficult. Hagar had to get out of bed early to lay out Sarah's clothes for the day. She had to brush Sarah's hair in a very complicated way. And Sarah stopped giving Hagar her leftover perfume and spices.

But it was more than that. Sarah was jealous of Hagar. She got meaner and meaner. Sarah made sure Hagar got very little to eat. She had Hagar beaten because Hagar served dinner cold, twice in a row.

Still Hagar continued to sing her song.

"Sarah can't have one
'Cause she's too old,
I'm going to have one,
And it makes me bold."

Sarah got meaner and meaner.

Things got so bad that Hagar ran away to the wilderness of Shur. She camped beside a small spring of water. She lay on her back and watched the ravens flying high in the desert sky. She didn't know what was going to happen to her. No one cared. She took off her sandals. The sand was gritty between her toes. Her future was going to be as hard as the rock she had put under her head for a pillow. She was a runaway slave. No one loved her. She had no food. She cried bitterly.

All of a sudden she heard a voice.

"Hagar, where have you come from and where are you going?" Hagar was sure this was a messenger from God.

"I am running away from Sarah my mistress," Hagar blurted out. "I don't want to be her slave."

"Go back to your mistress," said the angel. "God has heard how you have been treated, and wants to save you. That can happen only if you return to Abraham's house."

Go back to Sarah's house, thought Hagar? Not on your life. She wasn't that stupid. Then the angel said something wonderful.

"Your son will be born there. Name him Ishmael. That name means "God has heard." You son will be the first-born of that house. He will have a future." Then the angel left Hagar.

Hagar was astonished.

"Can it be that I have seen the One who sees me?" she asked herself in disbelief. Hagar could hardly believe that God had really seen her, a poor slave woman. She named God "The One who sees me."

She knelt beside the spring and bathed her face. From her cupped hands she drank the cool water. It felt and tasted so good! She called the spring "The Well of One who Lives and Sees Me."

Then she put on her sandals and headed back to Sarah and Abraham's house.

Her heart sang with hope.

"I'm going to have one, and it makes me bold!"

God Hears
Genesis 21:1–21

Hagar does bear a child whom she calls Ishmael. Ishmael cannot be erased from history, and will also demand his rights as the first-born and legitimate son of Abraham.

In the meantime, Sarah too has had a baby, called Isaac. It is a familiar scenario. The domestic servant (Hagar) is thrown out of the house by her mistress (Sarah) because she is pregnant by her master (Abraham). Sarah does not want the slave girl's son Ishmael sharing the inheritance with her son Isaac. By law, Ishmael, the child of a mere slave, is counted as Abraham's legitimate son. His presence is a threat to Sarah's place and the place of her children in the patriarchal household. No wonder Sarah makes Abraham force Hagar out of the household. Although he sends Hagar away with the child on her shoulder, he gives her some food and a skin of water.

Hagar has no way to correct the injustice done to her.

She wanders about in the wilderness of Beersheba, disoriented and displaced. She is now powerless **and** homeless. Both she and her child are on the brink of death. She places the child, who is dying from thirst, under a bush in the shade, and retreats about a "bowshot away" so she won't have to hear him cry or see him die.

At first God responds to the crying of the male child, not to the exiled woman's bitter weeping! An angel intervenes once again, to say that God has heard the child crying. The angel reminds Hagar that God plans to make of Ishmael a great nation. Hagar's pride, sense of dignity and courage are restored. God begins to seem more like the liberator of the oppressed. Maybe God hears the cry of all who have been wronged. Hagar begins to hope.

"God opened her eyes and she saw a well full of water." (Genesis 21:19) Water is the source and sustainer of life. Hagar the victim, the foreigner, the homeless and powerless one, was led by God to the wellsprings of life itself.

God Hears

We know a God who sees,
We know a God who hears
The crying of a helpless child
Will put to rest all fears.

Hagar went back to Abraham's house. She had a baby. She named him Ishmael, which means "God hears." Now Sarah also had a baby. She called him Isaac.

On the day Isaac was weaned, Abraham gave a feast for his baby son. Ishmael laughed and played with the baby Isaac. He accidentally knocked over Isaac's tower of blocks and Isaac cried. Sarah saw Ishmael laugh at him. She was furious.

"Drive out that foreign slave girl and her son," she screamed at Abraham. "I will not have that slave girl's son sharing your money and your name and your importance with my son Isaac."

She wouldn't even call Ishmael by name.

Abraham got up early the next morning while Sarah was still sleeping. He felt sorry for Hagar. He gave Hagar some food and a waterskin of water, set the child Ishmael on her shoulder, and sent her away.

Hagar and Ishmael wandered about in the wilderness, not knowing what to do. She could smell jackals. It was so hot. Finally the water ran out. She put Ishmael under a bush for shade. Strange noises startled her. Not another living thing moved.

Hagar knew they would both die if there was no water.

"How can I watch my child die?" she moaned. She went off about two bowshots away so she couldn't see Ishmael and sat down by herself. She held her head in her hands. She rocked back and forth on her heels, and cried bitter tears. Ishmael whimpered and cried too.

Then Hagar heard him howl.

Suddenly an angel came to her and said, "What is the matter Hagar? Don't be afraid. God hears your baby crying. Get up and go to him."

Hagar could hardly believe her ears. She stopped sobbing. She stood up. She ran over to where Ishmael lay under the bush. She pulled Ishmael up with her strong hands. She hugged him.

"God will make of him a great nation," the angel said.

She looked around and saw a well. She certainly hadn't noticed it before. But it was there now, so she went to it, filled her waterskin and gave Ishmael a drink. He smiled his tender smile and she smiled back.

They stayed in the wilderness until Ishmael grew up. He learned the ways of the jackals and ravens. He became an archer, and his bowshots were strong and true. His arrows landed far beyond the bush under which she had placed him when they first came to the wilderness. Hagar found him a wife from Egypt. And Ishmael became known as the father of the desert peoples, called Arabs.

Reversal of Values

Belief in Yahweh as a God of surprises, as a God of reversals, is one of the most enduring themes of Judeo-Christian thought. This God of surprises is evident at a personal level and at a communal or societal level. At the personal level, the barren woman is made fertile, the son of God is born in a barn and crucified on a cross. At the societal level, valleys shall be exalted and hills made low, and everything will appear in a different light.

The following stories are of women who, through their own experience of God's actions in their lives, came to understand God's action in history. They recognized a God whose actions reversed the values of the dominant society. As surprising as the barren woman made fertile, is God's action to fill the hungry with good things and send the rich away with nothing.

A God of Surprises (Hannah)
1 Samuel 1–2

This is the story of Hannah, a woman who had no children because "Yahweh closed her womb." At the time this was written, Israelite women had little status unless they produced offspring. To be barren was a curse of God and a woman's greatest tragedy. To bear many children was a sign of Yahweh's blessing. Hannah was not only barren. She was derided by her competitor, her husband's other wife Peninnah, who was able to bear children.

Hannah decided to address her prayers for children directly to Yahweh, rather than appeal to either the priest Eli or her husband Elkanah. Neither of them understood the depths of her misery. Once, when Hannah prayed at the temple, Eli thought her drunk (1:14). Elkanah's repeated questions to her (1 Samuel 1:8), including his "Am I not more to you than ten sons," indicate his concern and love for Hannah, but also indicate his lack of understanding of the unhappiness her infertility caused her.

Hannah vowed that if God would grant her a child, she would dedicate him to God for his whole life. It should not surprise us that Hannah herself made a vow. We have evidence that women in Israel made religious vows (Numbers 30:4–17) where there are provisions for how and when a husband could object. Her vow was, however, evidence of a spiritually independent woman.

Yahweh does open Hannah's womb, and she does dedicate the boy Samuel to God's service. Yet I add a word of caution. Not every woman who prays for a child receives one. The accent in this story is not on Hannah's child as a reward for prayer. The story must not be told in a way that suggests that God grants a child to every woman who prays for one. That is to miss the point.

The story is about how Hannah's experience of moving from barrenness to fertility gifts her with insight into God's intention to reverse things as they are. This is reflected in her song/prayer in 2:1–10. Although her song/prayer was not an original part of the narrative, the tone and motif of the prayer is not alien to Hannah's story. Its main focus is the reversal of fortune – for the barren women, for the poor, for the rich and mighty. Grateful for God's action in her life, she understands it as a paradigm of God's action in history. The overturning of the status quo between a previously childless woman and a woman who had many children (verse 5b) are not treated separately from other issues, such as the outcome of a battle (verse 1), the fate of the strong (verses 4–5a), the raising of the dead to life (verse 6), and the reversal of the fortunes of the poor (verse 8). The emphasis is on the God who surprises!

Note the close similarities of Hannah's prayer of reversals to the *Magnificat*, the song of Mary, the Mother of Jesus (Luke 1:46–55). Read it. The God who Hannah understands as one who grants fertility to the barren and justice to the poor is in continuity with Mary's God, who "fills the hungry with good things, and sends the rich empty, away." To have come to these insights Hannah must have been intimately acquainted with the poor. Perhaps she herself was poor.

Those who today pray her prayer, do so out of their knowledge of the world's poor. They long for a reversal in the fortunes of the poor and an end to the unequal distribution of resources.

Namibia, a poor country adjacent to South Africa, finally received its independence in 1991 after 70 years of illegal rule by South Africa, and having its rich resources plundered. Archbishop Desmond Tutu, addressing people at the national service of Thanksgiving, said, "God surprised us again. We thought this would never happen. But God knew it could." He saw God's hand in the reversal of Namibia's fortunes.

We tell Hannah's story so that the reader and the child will learn to recognize the God of surprises in their own experience.

For Further Reading

Fuchs, Esther. "The Literary Characterization of Mothers and Sexual Politics in the Hebrew Bible." In *Feminist Perspectives on Biblical Scholarship*, Adela Yaboro Collins, ed., California Scholars Press, 1985, p. 125.

Hackett, Jo Ann. "Samuel 1–2." In *The Women's Bible Commentary*, Carol A. Newsom and Sharon H. Ringe eds., Westminster/John Knox Press, 1992.

A God of Surprises (Hannah)

Walking on the ceiling,
What a crazy clown!
A most surprising feeling,
Being upside down!

If Hannah had a child,
Then dragons can be mild.
If lion and lamb together lie,
The poor are lifted high.

There once lived a woman called Hannah. She had no child, although she longed for one. Her neighbor was poor, and was always hungry. The two friends talked only of children and food. They would sing,

"A baby would be quite a switch,

Just like the poor becoming rich."

Hannah wanted a son so badly that sometimes she could hardly eat for thinking about it. She cried bitterly. She sobbed. She moaned.

Once when she was in tears and could not eat, her husband asked her lovingly, "Am I not more to you than ten sons?"

"No," thought Hannah to herself. "I love him. But I still want a son."

Her husband had another wife. She had borne many sons and daughters. She teased Hannah and made fun of her for not being able to bear a child. It made Hannah long even more for a baby. In her misery, she would seek out her neighbor, who longed for food as much as Hannah wanted a child. They would sing together quietly,

"A baby would be quite a switch,

Just like the poor becoming rich."

Once, when she was crying bitterly and eating nothing, her husband asked, "Hannah, why are you crying? Why are you so heartbroken?"

Hannah wasn't able to answer him, she was so miserable. She stood up, deeply upset, and sobbed bitterly. She went to the temple alone to pray to God. She made a vow, a promise. If God would give her a child, she would give that child back to God's service in the temple for his whole life. She went on praying for a long time. She stayed after everyone else had gone. She prayed silently, and although her voice could not be heard, her lips moved. Eli the temple priest watched her. Finally he could stand it no longer. He scolded her.

"Enough of this drunken behavior. Go away until the wine has worn off!"

"No sir," she answered. "I have drunk no wine or strong drink. I have been pouring out my heart to God. I am not drunk. All this time I have been speaking to God of my grief and misery."

Eli knew he had been wrong. He spoke to her kindly.

"Go in peace, and may God answer your prayer." After his gentle words she felt better. She ate something for the first time in days.

She left the temple and visited her neighbor who was poor.

Hannah told her about her vow. Then she shared her food with her. Together they hummed quietly their favorite song,

"A baby would be quite a switch,

Just like the poor becoming rich."

What a surprise it was later, when God blessed Hannah with a baby boy.

She laughed with delight.

She giggled in excitement.

She chortled with glee.

She rushed to tell her neighbor.

She dashed to tell her husband's other wife.

What a surprise! It was like having Christmas in June. It was like having Spring in December. "Quite a switch," her neighbor said.

She called the baby Samuel. She nursed him at home. She loved him dearly. When she had weaned him, she remembered her promise. She took him to the temple. He was to serve God all the days of his life. Her heart broke as she left him there, but she had promised.

She thought a lot about what had happened to her. How God had surprised her!

If she had a "her" or a "him," then dinosaurs could surely swim!

If God surprised her with a son, then God could surely feed everyone!

How surprising God was! She hummed the song she and her neighbor used to sing before Samuel was born, but with these words,

"A baby boy is quite a switch,

Just like the poor becoming rich."

Talk about surprises! It sounded as if God could turn everything upside down. Hannah knew that was true. She hoped that her neighbor who was hungry, would soon have lots and lots to eat.

No Room for "Them"
Luke 1:26–2:7

For decades, Protestants have largely ignored Mary (except for Christmas pageants, which usually present her as an angelic Madonna in a blue cloak). Recently, Protestant women have been learning a great deal about Mary from their Asian and Latin American Catholic female colleagues. It is now recognized that Mary is the mother of *all* Christian traditions. Thus it is the task of women of *all* traditions to redefine her.

Tradition has presented Mary as a passive and submissive "'hand-maiden of the Lord." This male image of ideal femininity has been internalized by many women. When this Mary is imitated, she becomes a useful means of domesticating women. She reinforces their subordinate position in family, society, and the church. More and more women today reject this interpretation. They understand her receptivity not as the passive acceptance of an imposed alien will, but as the free choice of a fully liberated human being.

Her "yes" to God places her in a biblical succession of strong prophetic women: women who connect the history of Yahweh with the history of humanity's liberation.

She stands alongside Puah and Shiphrah, the Hebrew midwives who defied Pharaoh's cruel decree (Exodus 2) and won the deliverance of their people; with Miriam who, along with Moses and Aaron, led the people into freedom, and who sings the oldest liberation song in the Bible (Exodus 15:20ff).

The names Mary and Miriam come from the same Hebrew root *marah* which denotes obstinacy, contrariness, rebelliousness, and revolt. It can also mean "plump and strong," which at that time was equivalent to "beauty." For 2,000 years interpreters have presented the "beautiful" Mary. Contemporary women are opting for an interpretation that can acknowledge the coexistence and complementary nature of "revolt" and "beauty."

When Mary sings her *Magnificat*, she rejects and disobeys the patriarchal order of things. This song reveals her hope for radical transformations, for life restored, for a new era, and for a life lived in harmony with God's will. Her song (Luke 1:46–55) echoes the song of Hannah in the Hebrew scriptures (1 Samuel 2:1–10). It bursts from the heartstrings of an oppressed people. So threatening is this song to people in power that as recently as 1981 it was banned from the national radio network by the military junta of Argentina. When, in 1980, Polish workers wrote on the Lenin shipyard walls the slogan "The Madonna is on strike," they showed awareness of the Mary who rebelled.

Traditionally, Mary has been presented as "up there," far removed from the struggle of people here below. In the Philippines, writes Hilda Buhay, "Popular prayers present Mary in a dazzling litany of praise – Virgin Most Faithful, Mother Most Powerful, Mother of Divine Grace, Mirror of Justice, Seat of Wisdom, Mystical Rose, and so on – an impossible model of life for us in our contemporary conditions," (*In God's Image*, Dec 89).

Challenges to the image of Mary as jeweled and elaborately dressed, as crowned and standing on the moon, are being issued by women of the Two Thirds world. Asian women write, "We reject Mary's hijacking by a wealthy church, for the consolation of the rich," ("Mariology," *In God's Image*, Dec. 89). "By exalting Mary, church liturgy, piety, and ethics have justified the continuing domination of women. But she is companion in the struggle," (Christian Conference in Asia, August 1989).

Latin American women see Mary's face reflected in the faces of their sisters, many of whom are undergoing the same pain and suffering that Mary endured, the same homelessness, the same experience as a refugee.

Ernesto Cardenal reports that peasants in Nicaragua speak of the need to depict Mary as wearing old clothes, like the peasant she was, rather than a silk robe embroidered with gold (*Gospel in Solentiname*, New York: Orbis Books, 1978).

Matthew begins his gospel with the genealogy of Jesus. This genealogy is of particular interest to female biblical scholars because of the women mentioned: Tamar the mother of Perez and Zerah; Rahab the mother of Boaz; Ruth the mother of Obed; and the wife of Uriah, Bathsheba, mother of Solomon. Why are these women named here? What do they have in common? In her book *The Illegitimacy of Jesus*, Jane Schaberg writes:

> All four find themselves outside patriarchal family structures: Tamar and Ruth are childless young widows, Rahab a

prostitute, Bathsheba an adulteress and then a widow pregnant with her lover's child... All four are wronged or thwarted by the male world... society was patriarchal [and] this caused suffering for women in certain circumstances... all four risk damage to the social order and their own condemnations... The situations of all four are righted by the actions of men who acknowledge guilt and/or accept responsibility for them. All show a significant lack of intervention on the part of God.

Traditionally, Mary's virginity has been understood *biologically*, which turns Jesus into a freak for contemporary women. We are not bound to think of the virgin birth as a physical event in order to believe that Jesus' whole life is of God. To read her virginity *theologically* is to affirm her as one of a kind, unique – the vehicle of the Incarnation. It is to understand the "Conceived by the Holy Ghost, born of the Virgin Mary" creedal statement as an affirmation of the mystery surrounding the person of Christ and the Incarnation. Mary personifies the people of God.

For Further Reading

In God's Image. Asian Women's Resource Centre, 566 Nathan Rd. Kiu Kin Massion 6/F Kowloon, Hong Kong.

Schaberg, Jane. *The Illegitimacy of Jesus*. San Francisco: Harper & Row Publishers, 1987.

No Room for "Them"

She had a baby in her tummy. Her heart sang.

She had a baby in her tummy. Her heart sank.

She was only 14. She didn't have a husband. What shame she would bring to her family! What would her friends say? She was scared.

She thought of her friend Joseph. She told him.

"Let's get you out of this town," he said. "We are all supposed to register in the city of our birth this year. It's a good excuse to go to Bethlehem at once."

She had a baby in her tummy. Her heart sang.

Joseph borrowed a donkey and they started on the long journey.

Clip Clop Clip Clop

Mary bounced up and down on the donkey.

They had no money. They begged for food along the way.

She had a baby in her tummy. Her heart sank.

How would they feed and clothe the baby?

Clip Clop Clip Clop

Would this rough journey ever end? It had started to rain.

Finally, they came to Bethlehem. Mary stood beside the donkey while Joseph knocked on the door of an inn.

A man came to the door and opened it a crack. It was the owner. He took a long hard look at both of them. They were very young. She had a baby in her tummy. They probably weren't married. Their clothes were ragged and old. They probably didn't have a cent between them.

"I'm sorry," he said. "There are no more empty rooms in my inn." He started to close the door. Just at that moment a well dressed husband and wife and their two little boys barged in ahead of Joseph. They demanded a room for the night. They looked as though they had lots of money.

"Certainly. Certainly. Come right in," urged the owner as he opened wide the door and beckoned them in.

Mary had a baby in her tummy. Her heart sank.

Joseph was stunned.

The owner, noticed the look on Joseph's face. He turned to Joseph and hissed, "There's no room for the likes of *you*. Understand?"

"But she is going to have a baby," whispered Joseph. "Isn't there some place we can at least get out of the rain?"

The owner looked at Mary. Mary didn't look at him.

"There's the corner of the barn," he said finally. "Just keep out of sight. Don't let the regular customers see you."

"Thank you," said Joseph.

That night Mary had her baby. She put him lovingly to her breast. She wrapped him in a warm cloth. Joseph laid him in the hay trough where the animals fed.

Mary had a baby. And her heart sang.

Saving the Planet for Christmas

The idea for a counterstory for children was given to me by James Theophilus Appavoo, staff member of Tamil Nadu Theological Seminary in Madurai, South India. He is an extremely effective communicator with poor rural folk. He has researched folk tales and songs as vehicles of the poor for social protest and societal transformation. One evening in 1990, he told me this story.

Saving the Planet for Christmas

adapted from a story by
James Theophilus Appavoo, India

You all know the Christmas story – the star, the sheep, the camels, the manger. Well, here's a Christmas story for our time.

A little girl heard that there would be no Christmas this year. She didn't believe it. There had always been Christmas as long as she could remember, and as long as her parents and her grandparents and ever so many people could remember. There was no way that Christmas would not come this year.

She thought, however, that she should make sure.

She went to the donkey who carried Joseph and Mary to Bethlehem and said, "Please donkey, tell me why there will be no Christmas this year."

"My dear girl," brayed the donkey, "there has been so much acid rain that the grass hasn't grown green. I've had so little to eat that my legs simply won't hold up long enough to carry Mary and Joseph to Bethlehem."

Next she went to the sheep. There was no sense going to Mary's women friends or to the shepherds. Their word was not trusted even in a court of law.

"Please dear sheep, why won't there be a Christmas this year?"

"Oh it's so sad," bleated the sheep, "The supersonic jets make so much noise that the shepherds can't hear the angelic choruses any more."

So the little girl went to the mighty camels.

"Please, mighty camels, Why won't there be a Christmas this year?"

"It's so maddening," grunted the camels. "There is so much air pollution and smog that the wise men can't see the Bethlehem star any more."

"Dear, dear," sighed the little girl. "The grass and the sky and the water and all God's creation is hurting. I would like to do what I can to help it to heal."

The little girl knew that there were some things she could do to help heal the earth. She knew about recycling newspaper, and pop cans, and jars, and plastic. Her parents had a composter in their back yard. Whenever she ate a banana, or an apple, or an orange, she put the peel in the composter instead of in the garbage. Months later, out came rich dark soil to help the grass grow green.

She was so excited. She thought to herself, "As surely as banana and apple peels can be turned into rich dark soil, if I do my part, Christmas will come again next year.

A Native Nativity
Luke 2:7–11

In her own intuitive way, elder Gladys Taylor, of Curve Lake, Ontario, paints a northern nativity with the imagery of the northern boreal forest, and in the context of the Anishinabe tradition. This story may remind you of the work of artist William Kurelek and his famous series *A Northern Nativity,* or of the *Huron Carol.* This story is used by permission, and was first printed in *Spirit of Gentleness,* the Lenten booklet for the United Church of Canada 1989.

A Native Nativity

by Gladys Taylor, Curve Lake, Ontario

A people who lived by a shoreline in wintertime watched northern lights filling the sky for three days, as they worked and gathered wood. Among the people was a woman elder who had a vision that something would happen on the third day.

Suddenly there came a sound like a storm rumbling; there was a noise like thunder – yet it was a moonlit night, the sky dancing with northern lights. In the frosty night they kept warm, close by the fire, the elder quiet and thoughtful. When all the animals began to bark and call, she knew that the time was near when a miracle would happen. Raising herself to her knees, she pulled the door of the tipi open. Her son tried to draw her back from the cold night, but the father said "Don't do that – a miracle is about to happen."

At the edge of the lake a woman knelt; the moon shining on the surface of the lake. She saw what appeared to be a white cloud approaching. At the center of the cloud there was a hole. The cloud moved over the lake and along the shore until it came to a tipi. It shone above the tipi for a very long time. As she watched, the cloud turned into a beautiful white Indian blanket with a small Anishinabe boy wrapped within. What had seemed to be a hole was the face of a child, dark against the blanket. A voice seemed to say, "This is the boy given to lead our people to freedom and to give us all that we need."

And that was the birth of our Jesus. All the animals, all the birds voiced their songs, each in their own language. That is why each Christmas all the animals bow down and give thanks to God for giving them such a wonderful leader... A lot of us have lost our language, but the animals and birds still praise God in their own language as God allowed them to do on that night.

A New Kind of Life
Mark 12:41–44

This story of Jesus and the "Widow's mite" follows immediately after Jesus' condemnation of the scribes "who swallow the property of widows, while making a show of lengthy prayers" (Mark 12:40). His teaching underlines the Hebrew scripture's emphasis on solidarity with the poor and God's value system – a reversal of the world's value system. The element of God acting in surprising ways is present, just as it was in Hannah's prayer (1 Samuel 2).

The women of Latin America have come to understand that they have been reading the Bible through the eyes of the rich and of men, rather than through their own eyes as poverty stricken women. They have also discovered that God is not neutral, but has made "an option for the poor." Their experience helps us to understand some biblical passages that are not crystal clear when viewed from traditional perspectives.

Latin American women compare themselves to "the widow who gave all she had – not worrying about what would happen next... They give all they have, their very life," hoping that a new kind of life will be born. (Raquel Roderiguez, "Hope Against Hope." In *Speaking for Ourselves*, Geneva: WCC, 1990.)

I told this story in a Canadian public school grade four classroom. I simply left out that *Jesus* was teaching near the temple, since identifiable Christian stories might be suspect in the public setting. I told it as a story about people putting money into the poor box. After the story, I asked the pupils whose gift they thought was worth the most.

A New Kind of Life

Clunk, clank
clunk, clank,
Clink, clunk, clank,
Of all the coins
dropped in that day,
Tinkle won first rank.

One day I was waiting for my father near the temple where Jesus was teaching. There was a box there into which people put money to help the poor.

As I sat in the sunlight I noticed a great big fat man come by. He was wearing a splendid cloak. He stopped when he saw the box. He gave his servant a lot of money to put in the box.

Clunk-clank. Clunk-clank. Clunk-clank.

It went on a long time. Then he continued on his way.

Next a woman wearing lots of sparkly jewels on her neck and a ruby ring on her finger came along. When she saw the box for the poor people she opened her drawstring bag carefully, took out lots and lots of coins, and dropped them into the box one by one.

Clunk-clank. Clunk-clank. Clunk-clank. Clunk-clank. Clunk-clank.

Another woman, dressed in beautiful purple silk with gold trimming walked by. She was in a great hurry, but she stopped when she saw the box for the poor. She quickly took two gold coins from her forehead band, to which each coin had been sewn individually. She dropped them in the box.

Clunk-clank. Clunk-clank.

Then another woman came and walked straight up to the box. She was dressed very plainly. I knew by her worn-out clothes she was a poor widow. She dropped two little copper coins into the box.

Tinkle. Tinkle.

As she was leaving the temple, I heard Jesus say to his disciples, "This poor widow has put more money into the box than all the others. They have put in what they could easily spare. They won't even miss it. But she, who needs coins for her own food, has given a lot of money to the temple box. She has given away everything she has."

Then Jesus and his disciples walked away. I wanted to follow them but I had to wait for my father. When he finally arrived I told him everything I had heard, ending with the part about the poor woman who gave everything she had.

"I was surprised to hear Jesus say that," I said.

"Yes. We who follow Jesus call it a new kind of life," said my father.

"Could we put some coins in?" I asked.

"Of course."

I wondered what sound ours would make. My father dropped his coins into the box.

Clunk-clank.

I dropped mine.

Tinkle tinkle.

Derhius' New Shirt

This companion story, *Derhius' New Shirt*, comes from Micronesia in the Pacific. It is based on an authentic story reported by Reverend Elden Buck, a United Church of Christ missionary in Micronesia from 1958–1986, and is adapted from the curriculum of the United Church of Christ.

Lorine Tevi, a Christian leader from Fiji writes,

We believe we are the church that has been called to live and care for more people than just our immediate family. When we do so, we acknowledge that God's new kind of life is already a reality among us. The new reality is often more visible in the Two Thirds world and in the poorer countries than in the rich churches of North America.

This story is about what it means to live God's love.

Derhius' New Shirt

Derhius lived on an island in the Pacific Ocean. Sometimes a ship would arrive from the District Center on another island. It brought food and supplies that were needed by people on the island.

There were four villages on Derhius' island. The villages were small. The fields were small. No one was able to grow enough food to feed themselves properly. Most people were very poor. No one had more than one pair of shoes. They looked after the few things they did own very carefully.

Derhius and his friends went from their villages to stay at the Christian Training School in a large town. There were 100 students there. Most of the students were so poor they had only two sets of clothing – those they were wearing, and those being washed.

One day the ship which traveled between the islands arrived with supplies from the District Center. One of the sailors on board was Derhius' older brother. He presented Derhius with a beautiful new flowered shirt which he'd purchased on another island. Derhius proudly showed it off to his friends.

A few days later however, another student named Manapu was wearing Derhius' new shirt. The school had a rule that students were not to wear each other's clothing, so the principal called Derhius into his office.

"Why is Manapu wearing your new shirt?" he asked.

"I gave it to him," answered Derhius.

The principal was very surprised. It was by far the most attractive shirt at the school and Derhius had been so excited to receive it. He had paraded around in front of all his friends and had grinned when they admired it. Even so, he had given it away.

"Why would you give Manapu your shirt," asked the principal, "when you seemed so happy with it?"

Derhius said, "Well I already had two shirts and Manapu had only one. So I gave my new shirt to him!"

A Symbol of Hope (Sarah)
Genesis 17:15–21, Genesis 18

Some find in Sarah a vindictive mean woman. Others perceive that she is herself oppressed. Few think of her as a symbol of hope.

Who was Sarah? She is known mainly as Abraham's wife. But let's look beyond that.

She was courageous. Did she not, along with Abraham, abandon friends and her homeland of Ur to pursue God's promise in the land of Canaan? She was elderly and childless. In those days, people thought that the childless – along with the lepers, the blind, and the poor – might as well be dead.

She was also wealthy. Part of her wealth had been amassed by Abraham at Sarah's expense. During a sojourn in Egypt, Abraham made Sarah pose as his sister because she was so beautiful. Pharaoh took her into his harem, and "Abraham came to possess sheep and cattle and asses, male and female slaves, she-asses and camels," (Genesis 12:16). Only later was Abraham's deception discovered.

In another story, we have told how Sarah abused her black slave Hagar. Like most people, she was ca-pable of oppressing others even as she was herself oppressed. But here, we tell a story of Sarah as a symbol of hope.

The words from Isaiah 51:2 about Sarah "laboring to bring you forth" were spoken by an unknown prophet many years after Sarah had lived. They were spoken to exiles in Babylon, to despairing Hebrew people who had lost family members, friends, homeland, the magnificent temple in Jerusalem, the monarchy, and the nation. Some thought they had lost God as well. "By the rivers of Babylon we sat down and wept when we remembered Zion," (Psalm 137, *The Jerusalem Bible).* This psalm provides a graphic description of how these people felt.

In 587 BCE the Babylonians cap-tured and sacked Jerusalem. They carried off into captivity the ablest leaders of Judean society. The tem-ple that Solomon had built was burned and destroyed. The king wit-nessed the execution of his two sons. Then he himself was blinded and led into exile in Babylon.

After years and decades, babies were born who knew nothing of

Jerusalem. Generations grew up with no knowledge of their own history, and no vision of the future. The exiles continued to be despondent. They had no hope. Then an unknown prophet, recorded in Isaiah 51, tells them an old traditional story from their history. It is the story of an old man, Abraham, and his barren wife Sarah. It is a story of hope, and Sarah, as the vehicle of hope, is the centerpiece.

Her story was an example and a model for the restoration of Israel out of the bleak and destroyed Jerusalem. If God could bring new life from Sarah, who is to set limits on God's creativity?

If the exiles had remembered their ancient stories, they might have realized that they were not the first or only generation to have given way to despair. This ancient story reminded them that God was present with them even in the midst of apparent hopelessness. God is a God of hope.

There is a legend, says Ginzberg in *Legends of the Jews*, that claims,

> *the whole world rejoiced, for God remembered all barren women at the same time with Sarah. They all bore children. And all the blind were made to see, the lame were made whole, the dumb were made to speak, and the mad were restored to reason. (Louis Ginzberg, The Legends of the Jews, Philadelphia: Jewish Publication Society, 1912, vol. 6, p. 262.)*

For Further Reading

Darr, Katheryn Pfisterer. *Far More Precious Than Jewels.* Louisville: Westminster/John Knox Press, 1991.

Symbol of Hope (Sarah)

Summer, fall, winter, spring,
but still no child did the new year bring.

Summer, fall, winter, spring,
Finally a new child God did bring.

Once long ago, there was a woman called Sarah. She desperately wanted to have a baby. What was life without a child? Without tender hugs, or walks in the meadows, or fun games, or wet kisses, or somebody asking "Why?" With no joyful noise, no happy confusion? She wanted a child to love.

So did her husband Abraham. He wanted a child to love. And when he died, he wanted to be able to give his name and his land to a child. Without a child, there seemed to be no future, no brightness, no light. God had once promised them that they would have children, grandchildren, and great-grandchildren – as many as stars in the sky. Sarah often thought of that promise at night when she would look up at the Milky Way.

Sometimes Sarah was angry because she didn't have a child. Other times she was sad. She was getting too old to have a child. She gave up all hope.

When Abraham was 99 years old, God came to him.

"I will give you a son by Sarah. She will be the mother of nations; the kings of many people shall spring from her," announced God.

Abraham was so surprised that he fell down on his face.

"Can a son be born to a man who is almost 100 years old? Can Sarah give birth to a son when she is 90? She's old enough to be a great-grandma!"

He snickered at the thought.

He giggled at the idea.

He chuckled at the notion.

He opened his mouth wide and guffawed.

"Whoa!" said God. "Don't you trust me any more? Your wife Sarah will give birth to a son and you will call him Isaac. He will have many children, and they will have many many children until there is a great nation of people."

Later, when Abraham was sitting outside his tent, three strangers came to visit. Because they were hungry, he fed them cake and milk that Sarah prepared. He waited under a tree while they ate.

Sarah was in the tent. She heard one of the strangers say to Abraham, "This time next year, in the spring when everything comes alive, Sarah will carry a baby. You will have a son."

She snickered at the thought.

She giggled at the idea.

She chuckled at the notion.

She opened her mouth wide and guffawed.

The stranger heard her laugh and turned to Abraham. "Why did Sarah laugh? Is anything too wonderful for God? You wait and see. Next year Sarah shall have a son."

And so it was. They named the baby Isaac, a name that means "laughter."

"God has brought me laughter" Sarah said. "Everyone who hears will laugh with me."

Her friends laughed with delight,
the blind people could see,
the lame danced with gaiety,
and the whole world rejoiced.

There were tender hugs, and walks in the meadows, and fun games, and wet kisses, and somebody asking "Why?" There was joyful noise and happy confusion and someone to love.

When Isaac was old enough, Sarah and Abraham told him how he was born. And the child whose name meant laughter,
snickered at the thought,
giggled at the idea,
chuckled at the notion,
opened his mouth wide and guffawed.

Three Women Warriors

The following stories deal with two of the bloodier moments in Israel's history: the beheading of General Holfernes, and the killing of General Sisera. No doubt many of us do not readily associate women with these kind of actions. Neither the actions, nor the women, fit our stereotypes of what is right.

But many of us may be distressed at a more profound level. Increasingly, people are developing sensibilities which challenge the use of all forms of violence, but especially violence committed in the name of God and religion.

Women have been at the forefront of this change. This is perhaps natural. Women have been and continue to be on the receiving end of most of the violence – physical, psychological, and systemic – committed in our society. We are beginning to speak out, attempting to put an end to the cycle of violence.

On yet another level, perhaps we are disturbed by images of our sisters acting in ways we have ourselves rejected.

Some might claim therefore that these stories should not be told to children. However, we do not tell these stories as morality tales, but as part of the story of women and men who unified the tribes of Israel. David's severing of Goliath's head was bloody, and Peter's betrayal of Jesus is anything but exemplary. Only when the full story of women has been told will it be time to raise questions about the morality of the actions of both Judith and David, Jael and Peter. For children, the story of David and Goliath implies that they too can be slayers of giants. In this story, since good and evil are clearly separated, children may get the same message.

Judith
The Apocrypha

Judith, a fictional character, was both a warrior and a femme fatale. She acted out both male and female roles. Her story tells how God delivered Israel from its enemies through her hands. She was a widow, and inherited her husband's considerable wealth at his death. She was free to reject suitors. She had the authority to summon the elders of the town or to rebuke them (8:11), thus fulfilling a male role. She was beautiful (10:7) and used her sexuality to defeat her enemy, thus fulfilling the female role. She lived to old age. Before she died, she distributed all her property to her husband's and her own kin. When she died she was mourned for seven days.

The book of Judith (which contains many historical inaccuracies and is therefore thought to be fiction) was recognized by the Church only after a certain hesitancy. Even then it was put into the Apocrypha, a collection of writings which appear in some Bibles, such as *The Jerusalem Bible*, but not in others.

It was written to explain the origins of the Feast of Hanukkah, The Feast of Lights (Rededication), which is often celebrated at the same time as the Christian Christmas. The feast was instituted to celebrate the victory of the Jews, led by their general Judas Maccabeus, over the pagan Syrians. In 165 BCE Judas Maccabeus defeated the Syrian general Antiochus Epiphanes who had forbidden Jews to circumcise, to celebrate religious festivals, or to observe the Sabbath. He set up a Greek altar to Zeus in the Temple in Jerusalem and sacrificed swine on it. After their victory, Jews cleansed and rededicated the Temple. The eight candlestick Menorah came into common usage.

Judith is a female Judas Maccabeus. Ostensibly the story details the defeat of Nebuchadnezzar's armies through a woman's single-handed assassination of their commander. Its main motif is to espouse God as the God of the Exodus: "the God of the lowly, the helper of the oppressed, the supporter of the weak, the savior of the despairing" (9:11).

The reader will recall the stories of Jael's bloody victory over Sisera (Judges 4:21) and David's beheading of Goliath (1 Samuel 17:51) as

Judith's story unfolds. Using her sexuality like Mata Hari, and her beauty to its best advantage, Judith went into the camp of her enemy Holfernes. Holfernes had laid siege to Bethulia and cut off the water supply. She pretended to be abandoning the doomed city and seeking refuge with the conqueror-to-be. He fell for her trap. He became drunk with her beauty and with wine. Judith beheaded him as he lay collapsed, wine sodden, on his own bed in the tent where she was alone with him. She saved her people by using her main weapon – her sexuality.

Elisabeth Schussler Fiorenza, in *In Memory of Her*, quotes from an authority on Jewish literature:

> Her use of deceit and specifically her sexuality may seem offensive... For the author it is the opposite. Judith wisely chooses the *weapon in her arsenal that is appropriate to her enemy's weakness. She plays his game, knowing that he will lose (p. 118).*

The victory celebration of the people, led by Judith's song and dance (15:13) is reminiscent of Miriam's song after crossing the Red Sea. Judith feasted with the people in Jerusalem for three months before returning home.

She is depicted as one who acted decisively, with wisdom and strong leadership. Christians have mistakenly sometimes pictured Jewish women in negative terms. The book of Judith tells a different story. The wisdom and courage of a woman saved her people once more. Clement of Rome, one of the early church fathers, once described her as the "blessed Judith." Here is her story.

For Further Reading

Fiorenza, Elisabeth Schussler. *In Memory of Her*. New York: Crossroad, 1983.

LaCoque, Andre. "Judith." In *The Feminine Unconventional*, Minneapolis: Fortress Press,1990, p 31–38.

Moore, Carey A. "Judith: The Case of the Pious Killer," in *Bible Review*, Washington, DC: Biblical Archaeology Society, February, 1990, pp. 26–36.

"Judith." In *The Anchor Bible*, New York: Doubleday, 1985.

Judith

adapted from
"Partners in Storytelling" group
Regina, Saskatchewan

God of the lowly,
God of the weak,
God of the victims,
That God, Judith seeks.

Everyone in Bethulia was thirsty. The water jars were empty. The wells had dried up. Each person could have only a small amount of water to drink each day. Children grew weak with thirst. Men and women collapsed in the streets.

Holfernes, a strong and mighty general of the powerful King Nebuchadnezzar, had surrounded Bethulia and cut off its water supply. The leading men of the town decided they could only wait five more days. If God had not come to their aid and sent water by then, they would surrender to their feared and wicked enemy.

There was a Hebrew woman called Judith who lived in Bethulia. She was very rich, and had everything in her house you could imagine. But she dressed in dull clothes, for she was a widow. For three years she came out of her house only on feast days and religious holidays. She prayed daily.

She heard how the men had decided to wait five more days for water, before surrendering to Holfernes. She called the leaders to her house.

"You were wrong to say we would surrender our town if God does not come to our help in five days. How could you do this? How could you test God in this way? Have you no faith?" she said angrily. "Let us wait patiently for God to save us. God will hear our pleading."

"We know it was not right. But what could we do? It was up to us to do something. The people were so thirsty," replied the leaders.

"Listen to me," said Judith. "I will do something that will be remembered by the children of this town and by their children and by children everywhere forever and ever."

The leaders wondered what she would do. She was only a widow, but they knew that even as a little girl she had been wise and daring.

"Tonight," she said, "my maid and I will go to the town gates. You must open them and let us go out. Before five days are up, I will return. You must not ask me anything about what I'm going to do. I won't tell you until it is done."

"Go in peace," said the town leaders. "May God show you a way to save us." They left her house, but soon began to scoff.

"She'll never do anything. She's only a woman," exclaimed one.

"I think she's bluffing," said another. "No woman can save us. Still, I wonder what she has up her sleeve?"

Judith knelt on the floor of her house and prayed.

"God of the lowly,

God of the weak,

God of the forgotten,

Help us now in our hour of need, or we will be destroyed by this enemy that stretches as far as the eye can see. Give me strength. Give me the tongue of a trickster to wound and kill those who are against you. Help me charm your enemy, and destroy him."

Then she went and bathed herself. She put on costly perfume. She fixed up her hair which was long and thick. She put on linen robes she had worn on joyful occasions when her husband was alive, and a tunic of many colors that shone brilliantly. She put on sandals, necklaces, bracelets, rings, earrings, and all her jewellery. She made herself beautiful enough to catch the eye of every man that saw her.

Then she called her maid and told her to get a skin of wine, a flask of oil, barley cakes, dried fruit, and pure loaves. When everything was ready, Judith and her maid left the house. They walked down the streets of the town, through the gates, down the mountain, and into the valley.

It wasn't long before one of Holfernes' guards stopped them.

"Who are you? Which side are you on? Where are you going?"

"I am an Israelite woman," said Judith. "I am fleeing from my people because they will soon be destroyed. I am on my way to see Holfernes, the general. I will show him the road to take if he wants to capture Bethulia without losing any of his own men."

The guards stared at Judith. She was such a beautiful woman. A crowd began forming around her. They marveled at her beauty.

"Who could despise a people having women like this?" they asked each other. "It is not wise to leave any Israelites alive, for if we let them go, they will be able to charm and trick the whole world."

"We will take you to our General Holfernes," said one of the guards. "Don't be afraid. Tell him what you have just told us and you will be treated well."

An escort of 100 men took Judith to the tent of Holfernes. The general was lying on his bed. Above it hung a cloth drape of purple and gold, studded with emeralds and precious stones. When the guards introduced her, Holfernes came forward in the tent, silver torches carried before him. He was astonished at her beauty, but made no sign. She fell on her knees before him.

"How stupid he is to believe this means I respect him," she

thought to herself. His guards raised her to her feet.

"Have courage, woman," he said. "I have never hurt anyone who serves my master King Nebuchadnezzar. No one shall hurt you. But tell me, why have you fled your own people and come to me?"

"My Lord," she began. "Long life to your master Nebuchadnezzar, king of the whole world. I have come here to seek refuge. I know that my people, who cannot be destroyed unless they disobey God, are about to commit a sin. They are short of food and their water is running out. They are going to eat the first crop of corn, even though it is against their own law. It should be sent to the priests in Jerusalem.

"When they eat the corn, they will be delivered into your hands. And I, through prayers to my God, can tell you the exact moment when it will be right for you to attack and destroy them. When I have done this, I will take you to Jerusalem and set you on a throne in the middle of the city, and no one will speak against you." She knew he would believe her because she was very beautiful.

"Israelite woman," said Holfernes, "there is no woman like you from one end of the earth to the other. Not only are you beautiful, but you are wise. You will save yourself by this action. If you do as you have promised, I will see that you have a home in the palace of Nebuchadnezzar."

He took Judith to another tent which he said she could have for her own while she was in the camp.

"Now," said Holfernes, "come and eat with me." He brought her to where his silver dinner service was laid out.

But Judith said, "No. I must eat only the special food my maid has brought with us, according to the custom of my people." Her maid opened the food bag to show him her special food.

"What will you do when your food runs out, for there is none like it here in my camp," said Holfernes.

Judith answered, "My food will last long enough for the task that I must do."

While she ate her own food, Holfernes watched her. He planned to trick her and make her his slave.

After dinner, Judith pleaded, "My Lord, grant that my maid and I can go outside the camp every night to pray to our God. That way I will know the exact moment when my people sin."

Holfernes agreed. So every night Judith and her maid went to the spring in the valley and bathed and prayed. She called on God to save her people from destruction. Every day she and her maid continued to eat their own food and drink their own drink.

On the fourth day Holfernes said to Judith, "I'm having a feast tonight. You will be the main guest. I hope you will enjoy my company."

"I would be very happy to enjoy your company, my Lord," smiled Judith.

Holfernes smiled slyly. "After tonight," he thought to himself, "she will be my slave." He spread the lamb's fleece he had given Judith to lie on as she ate. They ate and drank lying on the fleece, facing each other, as was the custom. He couldn't take his eyes off Judith, she was so beautiful. There was plenty to eat and lots to drink. Holfernes ate, and ate, and drank, and drank. He drank more wine than he had ever drunk in his life.

"Drink, drink. Enjoy yourself," urged Holfernes. He planned to get Judith drunk.

Judith said, "I will drink and be merry. Today my life means more to me than any other day since I was born." But, she was careful not to drink too much.

Holfernes' slaves left them alone. He kept eating and drinking until he collapsed, drunk, on his bed. He snored noisily as Judith got up from the lamb fleece and went to the head of the bed. Hanging beside the bed was a large sword. Judith took the sword in her hand and made one last silent prayer. She prayed for strength from the God of the lowly, the God of the weak, the God of the forgotten.

With two swift strokes on Holfernes' neck, she cut off his head. She pushed his body down in the bed and hid it under the drapes. She gave Holfernes' head to her maid, who put it in their food bag. Then they left the camp together, as they always did at night when they went to pray. No one challenged them. Once they were out of the camp, they headed straight for Bethulia.

When they reached the town, Judith shouted to the Israelite guards, "Open the gates! Open the gates!"

Hearing her voice, the guards threw open the gates. Everyone was surprised to see her again.

"Praise God, who has saved us from our enemies," shouted Judith. She took Holfernes' head out of the food bag and held it high over her head. "This is the head of Holfernes," she cried, "general of the Assyrian army. God has struck him down by the hand of a woman."

"We can hardly believe it! Such courage!" cried the leaders of the town. "Your name, Judith, will never die."

Then the women came and clasped Judith by her hands and hugged her. "You have saved us. You have saved the babies. You have saved the mothers. You have saved the fathers. You have saved the cattle, the sheep, the donkeys."

They put wreaths of olives on their heads and sang and danced.

"Praise to the God of the lowly, the God of the weak, the God of the forgotten."

The celebration went on for 90 days. No one ever again hurt the Israelites during the lifetime of Judith, or for a long time after her death.

A Mother in Israel (Deborah)
Judges 4–5

Deborah and Jael are two fearless women leaders portrayed in the book of Judges. The stories illustrate the significant role women played in Israel's life of faith and in its military victories. This perspective is all too often minimized or ignored. That is why we include their stories, which should be told together.

For many years the people of Israel succumbed to idolatry. As a result, they fell under the power of their enemies. The book of Judges contains stories of respected elders and warriors, "judges" who provide leadership and call the people back to faithfulness to God. Perhaps you know the stories of Gideon the warrior, Samson the strong man, or Jephthah who sacrificed his only daughter to keep the vow he had made to God. The book of Judges portrays 12 such persons, but Deborah is the only woman judge.

The biblical record identifies Deborah as one of four women prophets, along with Miriam, Huldah and Noadiah. She is a versatile woman who plays the role of judge, administrator, military leader, singer, and poet. She is a strongly independent woman. The rabbis nicknamed her "the hornet" or "buzzing bee" because she seemed arrogant to them. Certainly she was spirited and decisive. She took up her role in history with vigor.

To denounce women for shrillness or stridency is another way of denying them any right to power. Women need to learn how publicly to declare their right to public power. Power is the ability to take one's place in whatever discourse is essential to action and the right to have one's participation matter. (Carolyn Heilbrun, Writing a Woman's Life, New York: Ballantine Books, 1988.)

The Song of Deborah (Judges 5) is a first-hand authentic historical witness from one who stood very close to the event. It took place about 1125 BCE at Megiddo, a Canaanite stronghold that threatened to strangle the main commercial route of the Israelites from Egypt to Mesopotamia.

God's participation in the battle makes the event historic and momentous. A terrific rain storm caused the river Kishon to overflow its banks, miring Canaanite charioteers in the clay. The storm is seen to be the sign of God's active presence as the leader of the tribes; the same interpretation given to the parting of the Red Sea in the story of the Exodus.

Deborah is also known as a "mother in Israel" although there is no evidence of her having had children.

Numerous commentators have praised her for her activity in the home (no evidence of which appears in the Bible, although she was married to Lappidoth). To have deserved such a title as "mother in Israel," she would have to have counseled and inspired her people, brought them liberation from foreign oppression, and ensured their well-being and security.

A Mother in Israel (Deborah)

Hornet stinging,
Victors singing,
Deborah and Jael
Save Israel.

(A story told by Barak, General of Israel's army.)

She was famous. She was firm. She was determined.

She used to sit under a palm tree known far and wide as the Palm Tree of Deborah. People quarreling over a piece of land came to her to settle their differences. You didn't fool around with her. Her word was law. What a woman!

She used to sing a lot too. They called her a "mother in Israel," although she never had any children of her own. But she was a mother to all the tribes. She brought us together in unity.

One day she sent for me.

"Barak," she said, "our enemies have treated us harshly for 20 years. They must be stopped. God has spoken to me and has commanded, 'Go and take an army of 10,000 men to Mount Tabor. I will draw Sisera, our enemy's commander, and all his chariots and warriors to the river Kishon, and there I will deliver them into your hands.'"

I was frightened out of my wits. I knew that Deborah was a trusted prophet. But how could she be so sure that God would deliver our enemies into our hands?

"If you go with me, I will go," I responded. "But if you will not go, neither will I."

I knew our 10,000 soldiers would respect Deborah and follow her, not me. I also knew that our enemy Sisera had 900 chariots of iron and many more troops than we had. They might defeat us. I needed Deborah.

"Certainly I will go with you," Deborah cried. "But the outcome of the battle will be different than what you expect. God will let Sisera our enemy fall into the hands of a woman, not you. The glory will be hers."

I didn't see how that was possible. All the soldiers were men. How could she be so sure that a woman would claim the final victory? Nothing like that had ever happened.

When we arrived at the river Kishon, we saw that it had become an angry torrent sweeping away everything in its path. Near the river bank Sisera's troops were lined up, the sunlight dancing on their gleaming spears. I was afraid. Then Deborah stood up in front of us.

"Up Barak, up. This day God gives Sisera into your hands.

God has already gone before you into battle. Take heart. Up Barak, up!" she shouted.

No wonder the rabbis nicknamed her "the hornet." She had spirit. Her words stung me into action.

The battle was terrible in its fury. Sisera's troops attacked us. I won't soon forget our chariots charging down Mount Tabor like an avalanche, the clash of spears, the noise and confusion. I smelled the blood of open wounds. The stars in the heavens fought on our side. We forced the enemy into the river Kishon. The strong current swept away many enemy soldiers. Their heavy chariots got stuck in the mud. I remembered how the same thing had happened when the Egyptians were chasing Moses and Miriam and the children of Israel through the Red Sea. God had delivered our people then and God was delivering us now. Victory was within our grasp.

But where was the enemy commander? Deborah had prophesied that Sisera would fall into the hands of a woman, and the glory of defeating Sisera would be hers. But Sisera had disappeared.

"Look Barak," one of my men shouted as he pointed. "Sisera has left his chariot and is running to safety." Since Sisera was the general, I knew victory would be ours if I could capture him. But he was too fast for me. I lost sight of him. I knew we could not claim final victory until Sisera had been destroyed. Who and where was the woman Deborah had said would stop Sisera?

But today the battle was ours. The tribes had fought together against our common enemy. Deborah and I sang a song of celebration,

"Dead, dead were Israel's villages,

Until you rose up Deborah,

You rose up, a mother in Israel."

Like a mother, she had protected us, and brought us together.

Jael the Foreigner
Judges 4-5

Barak successfully accomplished his mission. The enemy army was destroyed. Only the symbol of that army, General Sisera still lived. But the victory could not be complete until Sisera had fallen into the hands of a woman, as Deborah had prophesied. This is the sequel to Deborah's story. It is the story of Jael, a foreign woman, who effects the final blow to the enemy's army. Both Deborah and Jael demonstrated extraordinary leadership in unifying the tribes of Israel.

Jael's actions are not what we expect from a woman or a wife in a patriarchal culture. She obviously did not regard herself as her husband's property, to be treated as he wished. She disagreed with her husband Heber who was loyal to Sisera and his commander, Jabin, King of Hazor. Normally one would expect her to protect her husband's allies – in this case, Sisera. But she contradicted these expectations and demonstrated that she had a strong mind of her own. She broke all the traditions of hospitality to a refugee. She acted decisively and unexpectedly when she killed the enemy Sisera by driving a stake through his head when he sought refuge in her tent. Whatever you may feel about such a bloody act of "betrayal" you must first deal with the fact that this woman, a foreigner to Israel, helped to save the Israelites by defying her own husband and acting independently. That is partly why we include this story.

Her husband, Heber the Kenite, was at peace with Sisera's King Jabin. He had defected from the people of Israel, and was something of a spy against them. No wonder Sisera expected refuge, and gratefully accepted Jael's invitation to eat and sleep in her tent. The conversation in Judges 4:18–20 allows the reader to think that Jael will protect Sisera. This is not the case. She is loyal to Israel. Although not a Hebrew, she helps to fulfill the word of God (Judges 4:7) as announced by Deborah. Her killing of Sisera is remembered by Israel as a brave and revolutionary act. God gives Israel victory over the Canaanites and their strong leader through a woman!

For Further Reading

Joseph, Norma. Lecture at El Emmanuel Temple, Toronto, 1991.

Laffey, Alice L. *An Introduction to the Old Testament – A Feminist Perspective.* Philadelphia: Fortress, 1988, p. 89.

Jael the Foreigner

It was a dangerous time. There were few caravans passing our tents. Travelers chose safer ways. My husband Heber had become a spy against the Israelites. I didn't go along with this spy business. It was a dangerous game.

One day, as I stood by our tent, I saw a man running toward me. He was panting, and stumbling a little as he dragged his left leg. He must have been hurt in the battle with the Israelites.

He needed to rest and hide. I recognized him as Sisera, my husband's friend. He expected me to save him. But as I said, I didn't go along with that spying business. However, I said to him, "Come in my lord, come in; do not be afraid." He came into our tent and I covered him with a rug and made him comfortable.

He begged for a drink of water. I opened a skin full of milk, gave him a drink, and covered him up again.

He said to me, "Stand at the tent door, and if anybody comes and asks if someone is here, say 'No.'"

I wasn't sure what I should do. My husband Heber would expect me to hide Sisera from the Israelites. But I knew they had won the battle. There was no hope for Sisera. He had lost, and my husband with him. I always thought it wrong to be against the Israelites anyway. Now was my chance to do something about that.

I took a tent peg, picked up a hammer, and crept up to Sisera as he slept. I drove the peg into his skull. He died immediately. It was horrible. Then I went out to meet the victorious Israelites.

Their general, Barak, came up looking for Sisera. I said to him, "Come, I will show you the man you are looking for." He went into the tent with me and found Sisera with the tent peg in his skull. The death of Sisera meant the final victory for the Israelites.

Barak was very excited.

"Deborah told us this would happen," he exclaimed. "She prophesied, 'The Lord will have Sisera fall into the hands of a woman. The glory will be hers, not yours.' I had always thought she was talking about herself. But she wasn't. She was talking about you, Jael. You have struck a blow for the unity of Israel."

The Israelites blessed me for the final defeat of their enemy. But I didn't do it to unify Israel. I did it to save my own skin. I knew my husband's side had lost. I do not want ever again to have to kill a man for any reason. I don't feel like the heroine the Israelites make me out to be.

I'm scared now. I don't know what my husband will do to me. I might have to flee for my life. I wish Deborah had killed Sisera herself. She is welcome to all the glory.

Two Sisters-in-Law
(Ruth and Orpah)

Better than Seven Sons (Ruth)

Ruth is one of four women mentioned in the genealogy of Jesus (Matthew 1:5). She is the grandmother of King David. She lived in Moab, a small territory lying east of the Dead Sea. So much hatred existed between the Moabites and the Israelites that one of the laws in Deuteronomy (23:3) states that "No Moabite is to be admitted into the Assembly of God." Moreover, Ruth is a woman, widowed, and barren. How then did she earn the accolade, "better than seven sons" (Ruth 4:15)?

Most commentators believe that this artistic tale was written in the fourth century BCE as a protest against the prevailing hostility to the Moabites, and the stringent requirements on the Israelites, made by Ezra and Nehemiah. These requirements forbade intermarriage. The book of Ruth advocates an attitude of tolerance toward people of other nations. The anonymous author has so skillfully composed this idyllic tale that the casual reader would never associate the story with protest.

The book assumes the reader's knowledge of the Hebrew levirate marriage whereby the widow's next of kin was duty bound to marry the widow. This guaranteed the survival of the deceased person's name and kept his land in the family.

The second sentence outlines the conflict in the story. Sui May Kuo, of Nanjing University, People's Republic of China, translating the *King James Version* for her Chinese students, puts it this way: "A certain man of Bethlehem of Judah went to sojourn in the country of Moab, he and his wife and his two sons. These sons married Moabite women."

In her *Venturing Into the Bible* (Nanjing University Press, 1989), Sui May Kuo says, "This sounds like, 'In 1946, a certain Chinese went to live in Japan with his wife and two sons who later married Japanese wives.' It would bring to mind the heinous crimes of Japanese invaders during the war that ended in 1945." What a betrayal!

Who is Ruth? Is she "a paradigm

of faithfulness, a puppet in the service of patriarchy, or a radical call to inclusiveness?" asks commentator Esther Fuchs. Feminist theologians differ about this tale, because Ruth is a complex character. I take the position that Ruth fits all three of these descriptions. However, here I have concentrated on her as a model for radical inclusiveness, since I believe this was the author's intention.

Scholars Phyllis Trible and Renita Weems, who are not blind to the patriarchal emphases of the story (e.g. Boaz in 2:5 inquires "Whose girl is this?" viewing her as someone's property) would agree. The intermarriage of two people from two sworn enemy nations is a sharp protest to the isolationist stance of the people of Judah. It emphasizes the responsibility of people to redeem each other. Ruth and Naomi knew hardship, danger, and insecurity. They worked to transform their culture and the people in it to accept a foreigner, a Moabite, into the life of the people of Bethlehem.

Norma Joseph, a Jewish scholar, points out that the name Ruth is the opposite of "Ruth-less." Ruth is the origin of the English word "lovingkindness." She exhibits more than ordinary loyalty (for whatever reasons) in sticking to Naomi, in entering a foreign culture, and in bearing a child who restores hope to the living.

For Further Reading

Bird, Phyllis. "Images of Women in the Old Testament." In *Religion and Sexism*, Rosemary Radford Ruether ed., Simon and Schuster, New York, 1974.

Darr, Katheryn Pfisterer. *Far More Precious than Jewels.* Louisville: Westminster/John Knox Press, 1991.

Better than Seven Sons (Ruth)

Naomi lived in Bethlehem, with her husband and her two sons. There was a famine so Naomi and her family had to leave Bethlehem. They hitched up their cart to the oxen, piled their few belongings on the cart, and climbed on. They went on a long journey and finally came to a far away country called Moab.

The people of Moab and the people of Bethlehem were enemies. They had fought against each other for years and years. Their grandfathers had fought against each other for years and years. Their great grandfathers had fought against each other for years and years.

Nobody from Bethlehem wanted to live in Moab. But Naomi and her family went there because the Moabites had lots of food: melons, grain, raisins, figs, lamb, and dates.

Soon after they arrived in Moab, Naomi's husband died. But she wasn't alone. Her two sons grew up and took care of her. Each of them married a young girl of Moab. But soon Naomi's two sons also fell sick and died. Naomi was now all alone with the two young women of Moab. Neither of them had children. After a few years Naomi said, "I am going to return to Bethlehem. There is lots of food there now. But you two young women stay here in Moab, in your own country. It is your home."

Orpah, one of the young women, kissed Naomi goodbye and returned to her mother's house in Moab. But Ruth, the other young woman, said, "I will go with you. Your people shall be my people. Your God shall be my God."

Naomi said no more and the two traveled until they came to

Bethlehem. Everyone was very excited about seeing them. The women asked, "Can this be Naomi who left here so many years ago?"

Now, Naomi had a rich relative, whose name was Boaz. Because the barley harvest was just beginning. Ruth went to his field. She gathered the leftover grain that was lying on the fields after the men had cut the crop. Boaz couldn't help but notice Ruth.

"Whose girl is that?" he asked one of his servants.

"She is a foreigner, a girl who has just come back from Moab with Naomi. Her name is Ruth."

Boaz didn't care that she was a foreigner. He liked her. He told his servants to leave lots of grain in the fields for her. He told Ruth if she were thirsty, to go and drink from the water jars his men had filled.

"Why are you so kind to me when I am only a foreigner from Moab?" Ruth asked.

"They have told me all you have done for Naomi since her husband's death. They told me how you left your own land, Moab, and came here to people you did not know before," said Boaz gently.

Ruth thought Boaz was very generous to her even though she was from an enemy country. When mealtime came, Boaz invited Ruth to eat with him. He told his servants to pull out a few ears of corn and leave them in the fields so Ruth would find them and take them home. In the evening, Ruth happily returned home to Naomi.

Naomi said, "It is good to see you so happy. Go to Boaz' field every day. He will take care of us because he is our closest relative."

Ruth did just that, and Boaz continued to notice her.

One day Naomi said to Ruth, "My daughter, I want you to settle down and be happy. Our relative Boaz will be at the threshing floor tonight. Wash and anoint yourself, put on your cloak and go to the threshing floor. Wait until Boaz has finished eating and drinking. When he lies down, go and turn back the covering at his feet and lie down."

"I will do whatever you tell me," said Ruth.

So she went down to the threshing floor and did exactly as Naomi had said.

When Boaz had eaten and drunk he went to lie down at the far end of the heap of grain. Ruth came in quietly, turned back the covering at his feet and lay down. About midnight, something disturbed him and he woke up. There was a woman lying at his feet.

"Who are you?" he asked.

"I am Ruth," she replied. "Now spread your cloak over your servant, for you are my closest relative." It was Ruth's way of saying that Boaz should marry her. The Hebrews had a law which said Boaz should marry Ruth because he was her nearest male relative. Boaz was glad Ruth had reminded him of the law.

Boaz talked with the men of Bethlehem. He said, "I do not want Naomi and Ruth to stay by themselves. I know Ruth is from Moab. But I wish to marry her."

"But you can't marry a foreigner. Jews don't marry foreigners!" Boaz' men didn't like the idea at all.

"That makes no difference to me," Boaz said. "I am going to marry her. I am her closest male relative. I will buy the land that rightfully belonged to her husband who died in Moab, so that his name will not be forgotten."

Boaz and Ruth were married. Later, they had a little boy. Naomi took the baby in her arms, put him in her lap, and rocked him. She wasn't alone any more. Now she had a grandchild, a daughter who had a husband, and a future. The women friends said to Naomi, "God is good. There is a new son in your home who will give you a new life." The women named him Obed.

"But," they said, "never forget that Ruth, who loves you and gave birth to this son is better to you than seven sons."

Her Mother's House (Orpah)
Ruth 1:1–14

You know the story of Ruth and her extraordinary loyalty to her mother-in-law Naomi. Here is the companion story of Orpah, whose choice was to return to her mother's house in Moab rather than accompany Ruth and Naomi to Judah.

The rabbinical commentary points out that the name Orpah means "the nape of the neck," or stiff-necked. Ostensibly, Orpah was being stiff-necked when she turned her back on her mother-in-law! But Orpah was obedient to Naomi. Yet she has never been held up as a model person as Ruth has been. Let's explore this story further.

Orpah is a woman caught between two cultures and two ideas of womanhood. After 10 years with Ruth and Naomi, Orpah has defined herself and her society in new ways. Twice in the story she joins arms with the other two, lifts up her voice with theirs, and weeps at the recognition of what they may all lose in choosing to part company. Society neither sees nor sanctions the value they place on each other.

Orpah would like to go with Ruth and Naomi to Judah. She starts down the road with them. That road represents a new way, intimate friendship, and the rich quality of life they have created together.

On the other hand, she knows that such a road promises little for a childless widow. It could be a dead end. She is unwilling to remain eternally faithful to her dead husband's family. She wants to live her own life.

Only after Naomi urges her a second time to return to her "mother's house" in Moab does Orpah change her mind – perhaps with reluctance and acknowledgment of her loss. But she is also mindful of a rich heritage waiting in her "mother's house" and would like to build on that.

"There is value in your mother's house – in traditional ways," says Naomi.

Once more they weep. Orpah is silent. Then she decides to return to her "mother's house."

What must have gone on in her mind on the road back? Is it true you "can't go home again"? What of her past would she want to reclaim? How can she return without losing what she now knows about herself, discovered in the company of Ruth and

Naomi? She will want to make a life different from her mother's yet at odds with many of her contemporaries.

Ruth's virtue was loyalty to her foreign mother-in-law. Orpah's virtue was to return to her roots to try to transform them into a new life. Both choices are "blessed by Naomi." Orpah's story needs to be known, since it is also the story of many young women today.

For Further Reading

Miller-McLemore, Bonnie J. "Returning to the Mother's House." In *Christian Century*, April 17, 1991, p. 428.

Her Mother's House (Orpah)

Orpah, Orpah, quiet as a mouse,
chooses to live in her mother's house.
Ruth decides to try a new land
Holding onto Naomi's hand.
God blesses them both.

There was once a woman named Orpah. She and her sister Ruth lived in the land of Moab. There was plenty to eat. Orpah liked to listen to the wind whistle through the cornfields. They lived in a large square whitewashed house that had been their mother's house. Their family had lived in that house for many many years.

When they were children Orpah and Ruth used to hide secret notes for each other behind a loose brick in the courtyard. Steps at the side of the house led up to the rooftop where Orpah and Ruth spent many a night watching the stars. Some nights they talked until dawn.

They both married boys from a refugee family who had fled from Judah because there wasn't enough food. It was very unusual for Moabite girls like Orpah and Ruth to marry Hebrew boys. Hebrew law forbade it.

Soon after the boys arrived from Judah, their father died leaving their mother Naomi a widow. After about 10 years, the two boys also fell sick and died. Naomi was left alone in her adopted land of Moab with the two young widows—Orpah and Ruth.

Orpah loved Ruth and Naomi very much. For several years they all lived together in the square whitewashed house that they had known as their mother's house. They spent many nights on the rooftop, talking and quietly singing.

But Naomi had wanted to return to Judah ever since her husband died. So one day she said, "I am going to return to my country because I'm told there is enough food again." Orpah and Ruth decided to go with her.

To their surprise, shortly after they set out Naomi turned, hugged each of them, and said in a kind and gentle voice, "Go back to your mother's house in Moab. May God bless you both and may each of you find a good husband." She knew that Ruth and Orpah would have difficulty finding men in Judah who would marry them. Hebrew men didn't usually marry "foreigners." Naomi kissed them both. Orpah and Ruth burst into tears.

"No," they said. "We want to go with you to your people."

Naomi tried again. "Why come with me? I am too old to marry again," she joked. "And even if I bore more sons, would you wait until they were old enough to marry you?"

Orpah didn't think it was funny. She felt very sad. She and Ruth cried and hugged Naomi. Orpah couldn't imagine life without Naomi. Surely she didn't mean it!

But then Orpah began to think about Naomi's words. She loved her mother's house in Moab. She remembered what a happy childhood she had had there. She loved that house. She knew all its nooks and crannies. She remembered hiding her precious secret things behind the loose brick near the courtyard. She remembered the steps leading up to the roof where you could sit at night and watch the stars twinkle. She knew it wouldn't be the same without Naomi and Ruth. She would have to make a new life for herself.

She imagined what it would be like, rising in the morning and preparing breakfast only for herself. At least there would be lots of food! But then she thought how pleasant it would be to stay in her own country and speak her own language, and live in her mother's house where her family had lived for so many years. She knew that Naomi would bless her, whatever her decision.

Slowly she went to Naomi. She knelt in front of her and kissed her hands.

"I am going to return to my mother's house," she whispered, tears almost choking her.

Naomi drew her to her feet, hugged her, and blessed her. Then Orpah said goodbye to Ruth. She wished Ruth well in her new life in Judah.

Slowly Orpah turned her face back to Moab. She started down the long road that would take her back to her mother's house. As she thought about her new life, she walked more quickly. Before too long, her step became bouncy. As she came to her mother's house she broke into a whistle.

What do you think happened to Orpah? Finish the story.

Three Queens

The following stories focus on three queens – Sheba, Jezebel, and Esther – who influenced Israel's history. These women freely and unashamedly embraced power, understanding it as the possibility of effecting change. Women have traditionally denied that they have power because they have associated it with unsavory things. The stories are included to underline power as a reality in our lives. How one uses it – whether for or against people – remains the key ethical question.

The Queen of Sheba
1 Kings 10:1–13 or 2 Chronicles 9:1

The story is a poignant portrayal of a woman who was a foreign female leader and almost certainly a woman of color. Along with Moses' Cushite (Egyptian) wife, and the Egyptian princess who rescued Moses (both of whom were almost certainly black), these three are the most obviously African women in the entire biblical record, according to Mercy Oduyoye writing in *African Women Doing Theology – Exchange* (Vol. 19, 1990, NR1). That's one good reason for including this story.

In Ethiopian tradition, this queen is known as "Makeda," who apparently turned her people away from worship of the sun to the God of Israel. In response to reports she had heard about Solomon, she traveled a very great distance to discover to what extent Solomon was worthy of the Lord's name. She verified the reports for herself and, according to Ethiopian tradition, praised the God of the Hebrews. She responded in faith and then returned home laden with gifts.

A widespread legend tells of Solomon marrying Sheba. They had two sons. The royal line, the legend claims, came down through Haile Selassie, the Lion of Judah, making the Queen of Sheba and King Solomon ancestors of the Ethiopian king. This also linked the Ethiopian king (and by implication, Ethiopian Christians) to Jesus, through Solomon.

In Islamic tradition and in the Koran she appears as a wise, believing, and good woman even though she was a foreigner. Solomon is described as a prophet who "has knowledge of the Book." He hears from his talking birds about this powerful queen. When she comes to visit, she finds his palace paved with glass.

Sheba is thought to have occupied the territory of contemporary Saudi Arabia or Yemen. The queen's visit to Solomon may have been part of a trade mission along the caravan routes of the day.

The story recorded in both Kings and Chronicles highlights the splendor of Solomon's court. Traditional interpretation has emphasized how impressed Sheba was with Solomon's court and his wisdom. We bring additional emphases: her initiative in traveling a great distance, either to create a commercial alliance, or to verify the rumors about him; and her "testing [of] him with hard questions." The riddles I have used are from Proverbs 28:3, 30:24–28, and 24:26.

Here was a woman who must have been exceptionally bright and self-confident to question the wise and legendary King Solomon. She traveled at will, and enjoyed enormous wealth which she was ready to share. She was also a "seeker" after religious truth. She pursued wisdom and was open-minded enough to praise the God of the Hebrews, even though she was a foreigner.

For Further Reading

Previn, Dory. "Sheba and Solomon." In *Union Seminary Quarterly Review*, Alice Bach ed., 50th Anniversary Volume, Vol. 43 No. 1–4, New York, 1989.

The Queen of Sheba

Gold and spices and precious stones,
Raisins and figs, but no cellular phones,
Sheba brought them – a mighty queen,
Such wealth and gifts had never been seen.

The Queen of Sheba, like an amoeba,
Shared her lore, and came back with more!

Trip trop, trip trop. The donkey was so slow. I had wanted to ride on a camel. But the camels were loaded down with more spices than I had ever seen in my life. I could hardly see their humps.

"Are we there yet?" I asked.

Trip trop, trip trop. We traveled for days and days. I was so tired of the desert sand, of the wind, of the mountains, and of moving every day.

"Are we there yet?" I asked.

Trip trop, trip trop. It gave me a headache. I could hardly wait to ride my favorite camel again. It's a lot more fun than riding a donkey.

I was part of the caravan carrying
ivory from Tanzania,
gold from the Rand,
salt from Somalia,
sisal from Kenya,
copper from Zambia,

and spices from Zanzibar.

"Are we there yet?"

My mistress the Queen of Sheba had heard of King Solomon's fame and wisdom. She was traveling to Jerusalem to test him with hard questions.

After many days travel, we arrived at the city gates. Once inside the city we headed straight for the largest building we could see, King Solomon's palace. Inside the palace I saw two great pillars that framed six enormous steps leading to an ivory throne. The floor shimmered, either with polish or with water.

While I stood staring at the floor my queen swept into the throne room. Her black face and dark hair looked beautiful and contrasted with the large yellow sun emblazoned on her white robe.

I had to hurry after her, but when I put my foot out to walk on the floor, I almost lost my balance. It was so slippery. It was neither polish nor water. It was glass! Obviously the king liked surprises. I smiled to myself. A good joker usually enjoys a good riddle. If King Solomon were as wise as my mistress had been told, then I bet he could figure out riddles.

The king offered my queen a chair overlaid with fine gold. There were arms on each side of the seat, and a lion standing beside each of them. Nothing like this existed in our land of Sheba. My queen gaily started asking her riddles.

"Why, King Solomon, is a cruel king who oppresses the poor like driving rain that ruins the crops?"

"Neither of them have mercy," Solomon shot back before she could take her next breath.

"Tell me, Queen of Sheba, four things that are smallest on earth, yet wise beyond the wisest."

Without hesitation she responded. "Badgers are small, yet they make their home in the strong rocks. Grasshoppers have no king to direct them, yet they march together. Lizards can be grasped by the hand, yet they can be found living in a king's palace.

"And ants are so small, yet prepare their store of food in summer," they repeated in unison. They laughed and laughed. Hers was a tinkling sound like a bell. His was a roar like a lion.

"You didn't know I knew that one so well, did you," teased Solomon.

He laughed with delight, his eyes twinkling with cheer. Later, I went off to bed still chuckling to myself.

The next day, I went with my mistress when they showed her around King Solomon's court. She was amazed to see the house he had built:

curtains white,

lots of light,

purple hangings,

harps a-twanging,

linen held by a silver ring,

all of the palace, fit for a king!

At table, our eyes feasted on the food:

pomegranates, raisins, pears,

piled up higher than the chairs,

fancy bread,

melons red,

figs and cheese,

grapes and peas,

leg of lamb,

lots of ram,

skins of wine.

for us to dine.

It was the first time I ever saw my queen at a loss for words. She just sat with her chin in her hand. The next day, she returned to speak with King Solomon.

"The report which I heard in my own country about you and your wisdom was true," she began. "But I did not believe it until I came and saw for myself. Indeed I was not told half of it. Your wisdom and prosperity go far beyond the report I had of them."

King Solomon grinned.

"Happy are your wives! Happy your courtiers! Happy your servants!" she proclaimed.

King Solomon smiled from ear to ear.

"Blessed be your God who delights in you. When I asked about your God, you responded. A straightforward answer is as good as a kiss of friendship," she concluded.

King Solomon laughed out loud. He knew she had just repeated one of his own proverbs.

Then she gave the king
ivory from Tanzania,
gold from the Rand,
salt from Somalia,
sisal from Kenya,
copper from Zambia,
and spices from Zanzibar.

The next day, we set off again for the land of Sheba. I ran out to mount one of the camels. But I couldn't even see their humps. The loads we would carry home were even heavier than the ones we had brought to Jerusalem.

King Solomon had given my mistress
pomegranates, raisins, pears,
piled up higher than the chairs,
fancy bread,

melons red,
figs and cheese,
grapes and peas,
leg of lamb
lots of ram,
skins of wine.
so we could dine,
and much, much more.
Trip trop, trip trop. The donkey was so slow.
So much for having a clever mistress.

Jezebel
1 Kings 21

Jezebel was one of the most powerful women in the biblical record. Today, in the popular mind, she is thought of as a lewd schemer, mean, Satanic, and nasty. The sexual image of Jezebel as the painted woman is often used to emphasize woman as the destroyer of life. She grasped power where and when it presented itself. Women were not supposed to want or exercise power. Women who exercised power were seen as deviants, manipulators, or at best, exceptions. She confirmed that notion by using her power to steal property, to murder enemies, and to manipulate her husband. Women's access to power, especially in the patriarchal culture of ancient Israel, implied the control and manipulation of men. Jezebel succeeded brilliantly in controlling both her husband and the elders.

Jezebel was a high priestess in the fertility cult of Asherah and was accused of weaning her husband King Ahab away from fidelity to the only true God of the Hebrews. That is why we see her negatively, mainly through the eyes of Elijah and the Hebrew people.

In naming Jezebel's sins (and they were many) her strengths are often overlooked. She was the daughter, wife, and mother of kings. She had beauty, wealth and self-confidence. She was a foreigner and if she had lived her life in Phoenicia, where her father was king, she would have been considered as important and powerful a queen as Elizabeth I of England. Her contemporaries thought her a fine person and her story would read very differently if the god Baal had been in the ascendancy. She did exactly what any foreign queen should do: she brought her own religion with her, she worked to extend her husband's holdings, she stood up to Elijah, and she demonstrated that Elijah could not control her. She understood herself as equal to Ahab, her king and husband. She met her death in royal style.

Although there are others, we tell only one story about Jezebel: the story of Naboth's vineyard. We tell it not to exonerate or rehabilitate her. We tell it because she was one of the few women of her time who walked the corridors of power. Unfortunately, she held the same values as did King Ahab. They used their wealth and power to trample the rights of the less powerful.

The rich and powerful King Ahab stole land that had belonged to Naboth's family for centuries. He did it at the urging and by the connivance of Jezebel. There was no redress. There was only the misuse of power. In the end, however, the God of justice was vindicated when the dynasty fell.

Native people of Canada read this story as *their* story. Land theft and genocide is their history. Their land was seized by the first white settlers, although native people had dwelt on it for centuries. Many of their people were killed, as was Naboth. They are now struggling to have their legitimate land claims recognized in Canada. They hope that justice will prevail.

For Further Reading

Laffey, Alice L. *Introduction to the Old Testament*. Philadephia: Fortress, 1988, p. 131.

Jezebel

Queen Jezebel was mighty,
King Ahab was a twit,
King Ahab took a vineyard
Where Jezebel could sit.
But both of them were murdered,
Now no one uses it.

"Why are you so gloomy, and why do you refuse to eat? Are you or are you not king in Israel?" Queen Jezebel mocked her husband King Ahab.

He had come home sulking. He laid down on his bed in the middle of the day. He turned to the wall. He covered his face with the blanket. He refused to eat.

"I want Naboth's vineyard for a garden," muttered Ahab. "He wouldn't sell it to me. And he wouldn't take a better vineyard in exchange."

Naboth's vineyard was right next to the palace. It would have made a wonderful garden.

"Are you or are you not king in Israel?" jeered Jezebel. "You can have whatever you desire." Then she commanded him, "Come, get up and take heart. I will make you a gift of the vineyard of Naboth."

But Ahab went to bed and sulked. He pulled the covers up over his head.

So Jezebel took charge. She wrote a letter to the elders and important people of the city who sat in council with Naboth:

"Proclaim a feast, and give Naboth the seat of honor among the people. See that two wicked men are seated opposite him. They are to accuse him of cursing God and the king. Then, take Naboth out and stone him to death."

She signed Ahab's name, sealed it with his seal, and sent it off. The elders and important people in Naboth's city proclaimed a feast. They gave Naboth the seat of honor. Two men came in and accused him publicly of cursing God and the king. They dragged him outside the city wall and stoned him. Then they sent word to Jezebel that Naboth had been stoned to death.

"Get up Ahab," urged Jezebel. "Are you or are you not king in Israel? Take the vineyard that Naboth refused to sell to you. He is dead."

Ahab took the blanket off his face. He could hardly believe his good fortune. He got up from his bed at once. He ate a big meal and drank a lot of wine. Then he went and claimed Naboth's vineyard as his own.

Meanwhile, God spoke to the prophet Elijah. "Go at once to Ahab, king of Israel. You will find him in Naboth's vineyard, which he has just stolen."

Now this was not the first time God had sent Elijah to Ahab. They had argued many times. Each time Ahab did something wrong, God sent Elijah to warn Ahab that he would be punished.

"Have you found me again, my enemy?" asked Ahab as Elijah entered the vineyard.

"I have found you," Elijah said. "You have killed a man and taken his land as well. Because you have done wrong in the eyes of God bad things will happen to you."

"Am I or am I not king in Israel?" Ahab boasted, remembering what Jezebel had told him. "Can I or can I not have anything my heart desires?"

"You have done wrong in the eyes of God. A just king does not murder and steal. You will die in this vineyard King Ahab," said Elijah. "Your sons will not sit on the throne. Your queen, Jezebel, will be eaten by dogs."

These words made Ahab sorry for what he had done. He tore his clothes and fasted. He hoped God would take pity on him.

When Ahab told Jezebel what Elijah had said, she replied, "I don't care. I am queen. I have done nothing a queen shouldn't do. Elijah's God may threaten me, but *my* god will protect me."

But she was wrong.

Esther

In the tale told in the book of Esther, we meet Esther, a beautiful orphan, and Mordecai, her older cousin. Their acts of courage, faithfulness, and creativity deliver the Jewish people from destruction during the reign of Ahasuerus, the Persian king (485–464 BCE). Most commentators regard the book as a fictional story. It combines irony, suspense, and drama in order to explain the origins of the Jewish festival Purim ("lots"). Jewish children celebrate it as one of their favorite holidays. Some girls dress up as Esther. They put on long flowing gowns, sparkling crowns, and feel brave and loyal at the thought that they might risk their lives to save their people.

Esther has been idealized, and in some ways, made better than she is. Ginzberg's *Legends of the Jews* pictures her as "perfect" (except when she assertively petitions the king). She is the ultimate Jewish mother who risks her life to save her children, through modesty, loyalty, and quiet courage. She is a paragon of virtue.

A critical appreciation of Esther is that of Itumeleng Mosala, a South African theologian. He thinks that the context of the story is feudal and patriarchal and that it implicitly condemns Vashti. Chapter 1 outlines the lavish court of the king of Persia, but never mentions the slave labor that built it. What is not said is more important than what is said. The issue of class struggle is suppressed.

Mosala thinks that the story focuses on the cultural and national survival of the Jews. The price of survival is to incorporate Esther and the Jewish people into a hierarchical and feudal structure. They buy into the ruling ideology and condone the use of forced labor on the "lands and islands" of King Ahasuerus. (Esther 10:1–3). Chapter 9 tells of the victory of the Jews. The chapter states – three times! – that, in the course of their victory, "they did no looting" (Esther 9:10, 15, 16). Mosala claims that this indicates the Jews adopted the prevailing ideology that condoned the slaughter of human enemies, but protected private property of the ruling classes at all costs.

Mosala also criticizes the choice of a female character to achieve basically patriarchal objectives. He claims that the gender struggle of women to be independently themselves is sacrificed to the struggle for nationhood. He draws a parallel between the Esther story and the struggle of black women in South Africa today.

How to tell this story for children? However much one may agree with Mosala, the story still hinges on Esther's initiative. She seized her opportunity with courage, and saved her people as a nation. In a position to in-fluence historical events, she engaged in civil disobedience, risked her life, and delivered her people from annihilation. She could have turned her back on it all. Esther also teaches us how to use communal prayer and fasting as a form of preparation for solidarity. After the whole community fasts for three days Esther is prepared to approach the king on their behalf.

For Further Reading

Itumeleng, Mosala J. *Biblical Hermeneutics and Black Theology in South Africa.* Grand Rapids: Wm. B. Eerdmans,1988.

Esther

Esther was a Jew,
The king was not,
She asked for mercy
And he saved the lot!

Long ago, the Jews were made captive and taken to live in the land of Persia. Two of these captives were Esther and her cousin Mordecai. One day soldiers from the king's palace came to Mordecai's house and said, "We have come to fetch your cousin Esther. She has been chosen to live in the king's palace with the other beautiful women." The king had many beautiful women living at the palace, and he was going to chose one of them to be his queen.

Before Esther left, Mordecai warned her not to tell anyone she was a Jew. If people knew she was a Jew, they might try to hurt her.

When the king saw Esther he said, "You are more beautiful than any other woman in my country. You will be my queen." He gave a great banquet in her honor, proclaimed a holiday, and distributed wonderful gifts to his people.

A proud and selfish man named Haman was the king's prime minister. He was so taken with himself that he ordered everyone to bow down to him. But Mordecai refused. Haman became very angry and decided to kill Mordecai and the rest of the Jews. Haman didn't know that Mordecai and Esther had saved the king's life and that the king was very grateful to Mordecai.

Haman went to the king. "I have a plan to bring money into the royal treasury and at the same time, rid our country of dangerous people. I will give you ten thousand talents of silver if you will let me kill all the Jews. When they are dead, I will take their money and put it into our treasury."

The king didn't care what happened to the Jews. They were only captives. "Do what you like," he said to Haman. "The money and the people are yours." The king didn't know that Esther and Mordecai were Jews.

So Haman and his advisers decided upon a plan. All Jews were to be killed on the 13th day of the 12th month of Adar. Haman issued this order to the whole country.

The Jews sobbed and groaned. Mordecai dressed in rags and covered his head with ashes to show how sad he was. He told one of the servants to take a message to Esther. "Tell Esther," he said, "to go to the king and beg for the lives of her people."

Esther got the message but was worried. She sent a message back to Mordecai, "I cannot go to the king unless he sends for me. If I do, he could put me to death."

Mordecai knew that Esther was the only hope the Jews had

left. So he sent another message to Esther. "Don't think you will escape death. You will be killed because you are a Jew as well. Who knows? Perhaps it was for such a time as this that you were made queen. Do not remain silent. Save our people."

Esther was afraid for her life. She wanted to help her people, but she didn't think she could do it by herself. She sent a message back to Mordecai.

"Call a meeting of all the Jews in the city. Fast and pray for three days and nights. I will do the same, and I will draw strength from knowing all the Jews are doing the same thing. Then I will go to the king. If I die, then I die."

Three days later, Esther dressed in her royal robes so she would look her most beautiful. She stood in the inner court of the king's palace where she knew the king sometimes strolled. The king saw her and thought to himself, "I did not send for her. I do not know why she is coming to see me, but I am glad to see her." He held out his golden scepter.

Esther sighed with relief. It was the sign that she could approach the king and speak. She would not be put to death.

"What is it Queen Esther?" asked the king. He loved Esther very much. He said, "Whatever you ask for I will give to you, even half my kingdom."

"If it please your majesty," said Esther, "will you and Haman come to a banquet I have prepared?" That seemed easy, so the king agreed.

The next evening they all enjoyed a great banquet. Over the wine the king said to Esther, "Whatever you ask for I shall give to you, even half my kingdom." Once again Esther asked the king, "If it please you, will you bring Haman to a banquet again tomorrow?" The king agreed.

Haman went home from the banquet, thinking himself a lucky man. "The king and queen like me," he thought. "Next

month I'll be rid of the Jews and everyone will bow down to me."
Just then he spied Mordecai, and he forgot all his good luck. He
was so angry that he immediately ordered that a gallows be built.
He intended to hang Mordecai the next day.

But on the following day the king and Haman went to dine
with Queen Esther once more. Again, over the wine, the king said,
"Whatever you ask for I will give to you, Queen Esther, even half
my kingdom." This time, Esther bowed deeply before the king,
and pleaded, "If it please you, your majesty, let me and my people,
the Jews, live. An evil man is planning to kill us. Please save us."

The king could hardly believe his ears. Kill Esther? Kill his
beloved queen? Her people? Was she a Jew? Kill Mordecai, who
had even saved his life? The king had forgotten about Haman's
plot.

"Who is planning this terrible thing?" he thundered.

Esther pointed her finger at Haman and blurted out, "He is!"

The king rose from the banquet in a rage and went to walk
and think in the gardens nearby. Haman fell on his knees before
Esther to plead for his life. The king returned and ordered Haman
to be killed. When one of the soldiers told the king about the gallows intended for Mordecai, the king shouted furiously, "Take
Haman away. Hang him on his own gallows."

Then the king took back all the letters Haman had written
ordering the Jews be killed. All the city shouted for joy. For the
Jews there was light and joy, gladness and honor. Esther had saved
her people.

Three Wives of David

To survive in the household of a king who held political power, a woman had to be bright, ingenious, and strong. Being the wife of a powerful male – whether his power was secure or not – was and is no guarantee of an easy existence.

Abigail the Peacemaker
1 Samuel 25

The first book of Samuel features David and Saul, with other men (Eli, Samuel, and Jonathan) playing supporting roles. Commentators rarely mention Abigail, David's second wife. If they do, she is seen as just another woman in the cast of females supporting David's career and politically useful marriages. She is introduced as the wife of Nabal (1 Samuel 25). While she is described as "beautiful and intelligent," Nabal is described as "surly and mean." His name means "fool." We anticipate that she will surpass her husband and we are not disappointed. It is Abigail's wisdom and courage that averts a crisis.

Traditional interpretation centers on the promise made by God to David through Abigail: God will make David a prince over Israel. Her words are the vehicle of God's promise. The rest of the story is little more than a setting for this promise.

Our story explores Abigail, the woman. She is wise and beautiful. She is respected by her husband and Nabal's shepherds. She is assertive and decisive in her actions. She seeks out David on her own, delivers God's prophecy to him, and deflects his anger. She disarms Nabal's enemy and meets David secretly because her husband's male ego would not tolerate a reconciliation. Yet she faithfully returns home to Nabal, not an enviable task given the nature of the man. She doesn't mourn when Nabal dies.

She is, however, a sensible woman. She initiates action to stop a violent confrontation between Nabal and David. She "stands tall" in her peacemaking role. We include this story because of Abigail's significant role in deflecting the conflict between David and Nabal. The story captures her great moment in history. She is her own person, having understood the threat that David and his men represent to the property and lives of Nabal and herself. She disarms David with her hospitality and vulnerability and impresses him by her common sense.

Abigail becomes a wealthy widow whose land and assets David consolidates by marrying her after Nabal dies. A widow was dependent on support from her father before marriage and her husband and sons after marriage. If she was not supported by a man, she would have no voice as there would be no one to speak for her. She was a nonentity. In spite of her marriage to David, Abigail continues to be known as a widow, a word derived from the root meaning "dumb," no speech. She survives without further speech in the biblical text. She disappears from history.

Here is the story of an unrecognized woman who acts with courage, compassion, and power to make peace between two men.

For Further Reading

Bach, Alice. "The Pleasure of Her Text." In *Union Seminary Quarterly Review*, 50th Anniversary Volume, New York 10027,1989, p. 41-58.

Hackett, Jo Ann. "1–2 Samuel." In *The Women's Bible Commentary*, ed. Carol Newsom and Sharon H. Ringe, Westminster/John Knox Press, 1992.

Laffey, Alice. "David's Female Saviors." In *An Introduction to the Old Testament*, Philadelphia: Fortress Press, 1988, p. 110–111.

Abigail the Peacemaker

Raisins and figs,
Let's do a jig,
Say yes to peace
Make wars to cease...
Says Abigail.

There was once a woman who was as beautiful as she was wise. Her name was Abigail. Every morning she awoke to the bleating sound of 1,000 goats and the "ba-a-ah" of 3,000 sheep. The goats and sheep belonged to her husband Nabal, who was very rich, and very mean.

One morning, Nabal ordered his shepherds to cut the wooly coats off the sheep as was the custom. A man named David, and some men who followed him, lived in the wilderness nearby. David and his men were hiding from King Saul who wanted to kill them.

Because David and his men had been hiding for a long time they were very hungry and thirsty. When David heard about Nabal's order to shear the sheep, he sent ten men to ask politely if they could have some of the food and wine and meat that Nabal had given to his shepherds.

David's men imagined how good the fresh bread and cakes of dried figs would taste. Their mouths watered when they thought of the refreshing wine in their dry mouths. They were so hungry and thirsty. They had not harmed Nabal's flocks nor stolen anything. Indeed, they had protected Nabal's property against others.

But when Nabal heard their request he exploded in fury.

"Am I to give the food and wine and meat that I have pre-pared for my shepherds to men I do not know? No, I will not. Who is this David? Probably a slave. Today many slaves escape from their masters and set themselves up as chiefs."

David's men returned to him and told him all that Nabal had said. David stabbed the air with his sword and stamped his feet, he was so angry. Then he shouted at the top of his lungs, "Buckle on your swords all of you. He has repaid me evil for good. I will not leave a single mother's son of his alive by morning."

Four hundred of David's men set out to kill Nabal and his fam-ily and shepherds.

One of Nabal's men sent his young son secretly to Abigail.

"My father says we don't stand a chance if David attacks," he said. Abigail could see the boy's stomach rising up in his throat with fear.

"There is no sense talking to Nabal about this," Abigail said to herself. "He won't listen. He's such a fool. I'll have to do something myself." She knew how hungry David's men were. She acted quickly. She ordered her men to assemble

two hundred loaves of bread,

two skins of wine,

five sheep ready to cook,

five measures of grain,

one hundred bunches of raisins,

and two hundred cakes of dried figs.

The raisins and figs smelled so-o-o-o good! She had her serv-ants load all this on donkeys but told her husband nothing. She said, "Go on ahead. I will follow." Down the steep mountainside she rode on her donkey to meet David.

Plop clop. Plop clop. The hoofbeats of the donkey echoed the frightened beat of her heart. She repeated to herself again and again, the gifts she was bringing to David.

At the base of the mountain she saw David and all his men approaching. She quickly got down from her donkey, and bowed low to the ground, terrified that David would use his sword on her bare neck. Her hands were clammy and cold, and she was sweating. Then she called up her courage and spoke to David.

"Let me, your humble maidservant, take all the blame. Do not take any notice of my good-for-nothing husband Nabal. He is a fool. He did not know how to respond to your request. I did not myself, sir, see the men you sent, else it would have been different."

David's mouth fell open. He was astonished at the woman's boldness. His nostrils flared as the most divine smells began to tickle his nose.

"M-m-m," he sighed. "Raisins and figs. My favorites." Sensing his interest Abigail pointed to her donkeys laden with food and drink. "I have brought you

two hundred loaves of bread,

two skins of wine,

five sheep ready to cook,

five measures of grain,

one hundred bunches of raisins,

and two hundred cakes of dried figs.

God keep you from spilling blood, or giving way to your anger."

David felt his anger melt away. It was unusual for a woman to speak out in this way to a man who threatened her husband's life.

"Here is a gift for you and your men from your humble maidservant," said Abigail.

With that, she beckoned her servants to bring forward the mountains of food.

"My Lord," continued Abigail, "I plead with you not to punish Nabal. Spare him and his servants. I know that God has promised to make you a ruler of Israel and will favor your family forever. When God makes all you do prosper, perhaps then, you will re- member me, your humble maidservant."

There was silence. David was still savoring the divine smells. Finally he spoke to Abigail.

"What a blessing you have been. If you had not come out to meet me like this, I would have killed Nabal and all his household and his servants. God has spoken to me through you, a peace- maker."

Then David accepted from her all the gifts she had brought.

"Go in peace," he said. "I will not attack Nabal or his house- hold."

Abigail returned home. Nabal was very drunk, so Abigail said nothing to him until the next day. In the morning, she told him what she had done. Nabal was so surprised that he had a heart at- tack and died.

When David heard this, he sent messengers to Abigail.

"Would she," they asked, "consent to be David's wife?" With five maidservants she rode on a donkey to meet David. Plop clop. Plop clop. The sound of the donkey's hoofs reminded her of her first meeting with David and loaves of bread, skins of wine, and five sheep ready to cook...

Now she brought only herself.

A woman of peace should be more than enough.

Michal
1 Samuel 18:20–29, 19:9–18

You have heard of King David. But have you heard of his wife Michal, who saved his life by telling a lie? Lying is not an admirable quality that we want to espouse to children. Why then, do we tell that part of Michal's story?

The story portrays Michal as a minor character who nevertheless played a significant role at great personal risk. Saul's kingship had been rejected by God. David was waiting in the wings. Saul, hopelessly jealous of David, wanted to use Michal as the bait that would lure David to his death. Once David was his son-in-law, Saul planned to place him in the front line of the battle against the Philistines, expecting him to be killed. Because Michal was a powerless woman in a strategic position (daughter of King Saul) she was used by David for his own ends. As the daughter of Saul and wife of David, Michal was used by both men as a possession and a political pawn.

The story is included, not to hold her up as a heroine, but to help children understand how few choices we have when we are placed in impossible situations. Perhaps children can relate to the experience of powerlessness.

Bible stories are not simple morality tales. They reflect the reality of human life, and mirror both the evil and the saintly in human beings.

Our story is about Michal the Trickster. Had she not intervened and played a trick on Saul, Israel's history might have been different. She cunningly used one of the few weapons available to her. She lied. We do nothing for children by pretending that every biblical character is "good." But nor should Michal be vilified for displaying wit, prudence, and courage – all attributes expected in a man, but not in a woman. Remember too, that she took initiative on her husband's behalf at great personal risk. She "belonged" to three men – first to Saul, then to David, and finally to Paltiel. She did what she could in a tight situation. She should be honored for that. The sequel (which you may wish to fashion into a story) is found in 2 Samuel 3:13–17 and 2 Samuel 6:12–23.

1 Samuel 19 tells of Jonathan saving David's life, of Samuel saving

David's life, and of Michal saving David's life. Why do we hear so much more of Samuel's and Jonathan's role than we do of Michal's? Her story deserves to be told.

For Further Reading

Exum, Cheryl J. "Murder They Wrote." In *Union Seminary Quarterly Review*, Alice Bach ed., 50th Anniversary Volume, New York, 1989, p. 19.

Hackett, Jo Ann. "1–2 Samuel." In *The Women's Bible Commentary*, ed. Carol Newsom and Sharon H. Ringe, Westminster/John Knox Press, 1992.

Laffey, Alice L. *An Introduction to the Old Testament.* Philadelphia: Fortress Press, 1988, p. 108.

Michal the Trickster

Michal was cunning,
To put in the bed,
A likeness of David,
Saul's men were misled.

Many, many years ago, there lived a woman called Michal. She was the daughter of King Saul. She was used to commanding people and to having her own way. If she wanted figs for breakfast and her slaves brought her dates, she drew herself up to her full royal height and said in her best royal voice, "Bring me figs." Nobody crossed her up.

Saul was a mighty king. He was green with jealousy that David, a younger leader, might try to become king in his place. They were enemies. Twice Saul had tried to kill David by throwing a spear at him. Twice he had missed.

Saul knew that his daughter Michal loved David. That suited Saul's plans well. If Michal and David got married, David would have to give his full loyalty to Saul. David would even have to join Saul's army and fight Saul's battles with the Philistines. David would probably be killed in such a battle. "What a smart plot," thought Saul. So Saul made sure that David and Michal got married.

Sometimes Philistine officers would come to fight against Saul's soldiers, one by one. They wanted to see who was stronger. David won more often than any other of Saul's men. He won a great name for himself. Saul feared David.

Saul got tired of waiting for David to be killed in battle. So one night, he sent his servants to watch David's house, and to be ready to kill him when the sun came up.

Now Michal knew what her father had done. She loved David and wanted to save him. She cunningly made plans, and told David exactly what to do.

"When it gets dark, you must go away and hide. If you don't," she said, "you will be a dead man." David had to sneak out through a window. Michal lowered him to the ground with a rope. "Plop." She heard David's feet hit the ground. Then she heard him run away.

Michal was not finished. She knew her father's men would come to her door shortly. So she got a goat's hair rug and rolled it up to look like someone's head. Then she stuck it in David's bed, and covered it with a cloak. It was a dummy.

When Saul's men burst in to kill David, Michal met them at the door. What would she tell them? She knew they were more powerful than she was. She knew she would have to trick them to give David more time to get away.

So she drew herself up to her full royal height and said in her best royal voice, "He is ill."

They never suspected she might try to trick them. They left and told Saul that David was ill.

But Saul wasn't fooled. "Bring David to me, bed and all," he exploded, "and I will kill him myself."

So Saul's men returned to Michal's place, seized the bed, and lifted it off the floor. Immediately the dummy fell out! The captain in charge banged his fists on the wall and threw the dummy across the room in anger. The men turned on Michal in a rage, furious that she had tricked them.

"You must come with us," they said, brandishing their spears.

Michal drew herself up to her full royal height and said in her best royal voice, "Nobody tells me what to do. I am the daughter of a king." But she had no choice. The soldiers were stronger. Finally they forced her to go with them to Saul.

"Why have you played this trick on me and let my enemy escape?" Saul demanded of his daughter.

Michal had calmed down by this time. She was scared that her father Saul might hurt her so she blurted out, "I had no choice. David told me he would kill me unless I helped him escape." Saul believed her! He knew it could be true.

David got away safely.

Time passed. David had been gone so long, that Saul decided he would never come back. So Saul gave Michal to be wife to Paltiel. Paltiel loved Michal dearly and was always careful to give her figs, instead of dates.

No Choice, No Voice (Bathsheba)
2 Samuel 11–12, Matthew 1:7

Bathsheba is one of four women listed in Matthew's genealogy of Jesus. She is listed as Solomon's mother, and Uriah's wife, thus deriving her importance from the influential men in her life. She is the mother of a king (Solomon) and the wife of a king (David).

Traditionally she has been depicted as a seductress who bathed publicly so that David would see her beauty and want her for his own. But read the text again. There is nothing there to suggest that Bathsheba was luring David into her arms. Indeed, David was in Jerusalem, instead of being with his army as he should have been. Looking down from his high roof, he spied Bathsheba, inquired who she was, sent messengers to fetch her, and had intercourse with her, "though she was still being purified after her period"! She conceived, bore a son, and was taken by David to be his wife. Who then, is the victim?

Her story, told in 2 Samuel 11–12, grants her no choices, and no voice. She never speaks. She is victimized by David, who rapes her, impregnates her, and arranges for her husband to be killed in battle so he can marry her. He stops at nothing: seduction, manipulation, and even murder.

Later, Bathsheba bore a second boy, Solomon. The story told here is the story of Bathsheba through Solomon's eyes. As he grows up, he hears echoes of a baby brother who died before he was born. He asks for the story of the family skeleton in the closet. He can relate to his mother's story, because he, a child, also feels he has no choice and no voice. Perhaps the child you read to can also relate to this!

No Choice, No Voice (Bathsheba)

Wife of a king,
Beautiful and fair,
Bathsheba had no choice
In mothering an heir.

Solomon was seven years old, but he still liked to snuggle into his mother's lap for his bedtime story.

"There were once two men in the same city, one rich and the other poor," she said. "The rich man had large flocks of sheep, but the poor man had nothing of his own except one little lamb. The poor man raised it himself, and it grew up in his home with his own sons. It ate from his dish, drank from his cup and nestled in his arms; it was like a daughter to him.

One day a traveler came to the rich man's house. The rich man was too mean and too stingy to take a sheep from his own flocks to feed his guest. Instead, he took the poor man's lamb, cooked it, and fed it to his guest."

"That wasn't fair, Momma," said Solomon. "The rich man did a wrong thing."

"You're right, Solomon," said Bathsheba his mother. She had tears in her eyes.

"Why are you crying, Momma?" asked Solomon.

"I'm not exactly crying, Solomon. I'm just sad for a minute or two. Come, let's get your milk and figs. It's already past your bedtime."

Solomon wanted to hear the end of the story, he didn't want to go to bed yet. He cried and complained. But his mother just put him down, got his snack, and then took him to bed.

As he lay in bed, Solomon remembered little bits of a conversation his mother had with her servant woman. "Might upset him... he doesn't know... nothing will bring his brother back... best to forget."

The next day, Solomon asked, "Momma, did I ever have a baby brother?"

Solomon's mother was quiet for a long time. She looked sad. Finally she said, "Yes you did, but it was before you were born."

"Tell me about him," Solomon begged.

"Long before it happened, your father wanted me for his wife because he thought I was very beautiful. Your father ordered me to come to the palace, and soon I was carrying a baby in my tummy. He knew I was already married to a brave soldier. Your father wanted me so much that he ordered my husband to the front battle lines, and he was killed. Then your father ordered me to marry him. I had no choice, no voice. Nobody listened to me." Her eyes filled with tears.

"Was it like last night when I wanted to stay up late and you wouldn't listen to me?" Solomon asked.

"Something like. It hurts when other people don't listen, I know." She continued her story.

"Then I had a baby boy. But he got sick and died."

"Was that my baby brother?" asked Solomon.

"It was your baby brother," said Solomon's mother. She looked

down at the ground and covered her mouth with her hands. She remembered how nobody listened to her, and tried not to cry.

"Why are you so sad, Momma?" asked Solomon, creeping up into
her lap and planting a wet kiss on her cheek. "I'm here. I'm listening
to you."

"Son," said his Momma, giving him a hug, "You remember the
story I told you last night – the one about the rich man who stole the
lamb that didn't belong to him, the poor man's lamb? Well that's what
happened to me. I had no choice, no voice. I didn't belong to your father, although I was going to have his baby. I really belonged to my soldier husband. When your father brought me to the palace by force,
God frowned. It was wrong."

Bathsheba hung her head. "Nobody listened to me," she said.

"God didn't stay mad at my father did he?" asked Solomon.

"No, Solomon," his mother said. "God loved your father, even
though he had done wrong. God doesn't stay mad at those who change
their ways. All of us do wrong things from time to time. Your father
tried to make it up to me. So we chose to have you!" She smiled a little.

"That's why we called you Solomon. Your name means "beloved of
God." Your father and I love you very much.

Solomon smiled and snuggled into his mother's lap. He would
make it all up to her.

Rebirth

For Christians, the Resurrection is the foundational experience in their faith journey. Resurrection is the root of many of the metaphors – new life, rebirth, renewal – that best describe the dramatic transformation of beliefs, values, ways of being, and ways of being in community which define the Christian pilgrimage of faith.

It was Jesus' women followers who were the first convinced of the reality of the Resurrection, and as Elisabeth Moltmann-Wendel states, this is where church history begins.

Lessons from Long Ago
John 20:1–2, 11–13; Luke 24:1–11

There has been more written about Mary Magdalene than any other biblical woman with the exception of Eve and Mary the Virgin.

Church history begins when a few women set out to pay their last respects to their dead friend Jesus. It begins when, contrary to all reason and all hope, a few women identify themselves with a national traitor and do what they consider to be right... namely never abandoning him as dead. Church history begins when Jesus comes to them, greets them, lets them touch him just as he touched and restored them in their lives. Church history begins when the women are told to share with the men this experience, this life they now comprehend, this life their hands have touched... Officially, church history begins with the mission of the men apostles, and officially, no women are present on that occasion. (Elisabeth Moltmann-Wendel and Jurgen Moltmann, "Becoming Human in New Community," *in* The Community of Women and Men in the Church, *p. 29.*)

There are many resurrection stories. The ones around Mary Magdalene highlight the transformation of the lives of people. These personal transformations resulted in a community that carried on Jesus' work.

Mary Magdalene was unique in her preaching, her healing, and her

---

relationship to Jesus. Legends of the 11th century had Magdalene preaching, baptizing, proclaiming the gospel, and acting as an apostle. By the end of the 13th century, Mary Magdalene as preacher appeared in a stained glass window in the Cathedral of Semur in Burgundy.

She is twice described as the woman "from whom seven devils had been cast out" (Luke 8:2, Mark 16:9) and has been depicted as the epitome of sensuality and sexual sin. There is no evidence in the text that she was the great sexual sinner that tradition claims. Augustine, however, promoted the idea, and European history, art, literature, and current movies such as *The Last Temptation of Christ* are shaped by images of Mary Magdalene as the fallen woman.

Her total, spontaneous, passionate, self-giving love for Jesus has been interpreted by some as the response of an erotic lover. To women doing theology out of women's struggles, such self-giving is rather a paradigm for authentic human community.

Being "a woman of substance," she brought together a group of independent women of different ages, also separated from their families and therefore thought to be morally disreputable: Joanna, and Susanna being two of them. The transformation of human life began as these women were set free for a new kind of life. We are part of that continuing community.

For Further Reading

Moltmann-Wendel, Elisabeth and Jurgen Moltmann. "Becoming Human in New Community," in *The Community of Women and Men in the Church*, C. Parvey ed., Geneva: WCC, 1983.

Lessons from Long Ago

story by Donna Sinclair

"Woman why are you crying?"
Asked Jesus of Mary Mag.
"It's not surprising
That I'm arising,
Don't let your spirits sag."

She ran to tell the men,
The news of his arising,
"Idle tales" they scoffed,
"If true, it's most surprising."

Only a little way farther, my darling. I know, it's uphill, and the path is full of stones. It's a long way, even for someone who is ten; two days on foot and sleeping out of doors where the wild animals can get you.

Why did we come here, when I told everyone we were off to the market? Because no one needs to know where we have been. Except you, and later your daughters.

Ah. Here. Just the way it was. See, here, this big stone? This covered the entrance. But when we got here, it was rolled away. No, I don't know how. But there were angels, shining in the darkness, and the white cloth, all rumpled in the dim light.

Listen, my darling, and look around you very carefully. Look into every crack and crevice of this rock, put out your hand and touch this, here, see where he lay, yes, my love, you must. Your old Grandma cannot make this trip again, and now the story belongs to you, and you must know it with your eyes and fingers as well as your ears...

It was early Sunday morning. Everyone had been very upset, my mother and father and my aunt Joanna, because Jesus had died. I was just the age you are now, ten, and small for my age, like you. You would have loved him; he was always telling stories and making people laugh. Sometimes he would tell stories that weren't funny, rabbi stories, to teach you. I always stayed awake for those, even after the other children had gone to sleep. My mother tried to put me to bed once, and he laughed and said, "Does she snore so loud that she will drown out our talk?"

"Not at all," said my mother.

"So could she stay? A child's wisdom gives me joy, even when she falls asleep."

So I stayed, wrapped in my mother's arms, warm, and listened to the grownups asking questions, and arguing and talking until the voices dimmed into a soft buzz in my ears, and I slept.

But then he died. I was sad. I didn't understand why the soldiers killed him, why the crowds that cheered one day screamed "Crucify him" a few days later. No, I don't really know, even now, why it happened. Maybe all his talk was bringing too much change, too fast. Maybe it was the way women were so strong in his sight and children important, the most important, even. Maybe it was because everything seemed turned upside down when he was around: the poorer you were and the more alone you were, the more he seemed to love you.

Anyway, he died on a Friday, and Joseph and Nicodemus – no, you don't know them – took his body and wrapped it in a linen sheet, and brought it here. Pilate, the Roman governor, ordered a guard, and that stone, that one, was rolled in front of the entrance.

And on Sunday morning, Mary Magdalene and Joanna and the other Mary were getting ready to come here with the spices for Jesus' body.

"I want to come with you," I said.

"You're too young," said my aunt Joanna. I think she always thought I was allowed too much freedom.

"He was my friend too," I said.

They all looked at me. So many years ago, but I remember those faces as if it were this morning. Joanna doubtful, Mary interested, and Mary Magdalene suddenly clear. "She should come."

So I picked up my share of the spices and carried them carefully.

But when we got here, there were no soldiers. And the stone had already been rolled away. We looked in – I had stayed a little behind the others – and saw that it was empty. Jesus was gone.

The others started to cry, but I had been crying for two days, and had no tears left. Mary Magdalene bent over to look in the tomb again. I was right there with her. That's when I saw the two angels, right where it had been empty and dark before.

"Woman," they said. It's funny they didn't know her name, being angels, but that's what they said. "Woman, why are you crying?"

"They have taken my Lord away and I do not know where they have put him."

And then I saw Jesus, standing right behind her. I opened my mouth, but nothing came out. I kept trying to say hello, or how are you, or something, but there was no sound. It was the way you were, when I surprised you last birthday, only ten times more. He grinned at me, like always. Then he gave all his attention to Mary, who had turned around. That's how he was. He seemed to be able to focus his whole self on someone. "Woman, why are you crying?"

he said. "Who is it you are looking for?"

She was very polite, through her tears. "If you took him away, sir, tell me where you have put him and I will go and get him."

Mary seemed to think he was the gardener or somebody. And I wasn't any help. I was still standing there with my mouth open.

Finally, he said "Mary," in that half-amused way he had when you just didn't get it.

"Teacher," she said, and reached out for him.

"Don't," he said. That must have been very hard. It seemed she wasn't supposed to try to hold on to him. He explained very kindly that she should tell all the others that he was returning to God. That was all. And he was gone again. And then we left.

Yes, it was all kind of strange. You're right. And happy, too, and comforting, especially for me. I had felt as if life was over.

Why did we come here?

So you could know the story. So you could know it was women who first saw the risen Jesus. Even me, a girl. The teacher Paul – you've heard about him – said that it was Peter who saw Jesus first, but it wasn't. Paul left us out of the story.

No, I don't know why he did that. Yes, it is important. You must remember this, my darling. A girl is as good a witness as a boy. A girl can tell the truth just as well. Jesus always treated women as if we were as good as men.

Anyway, that's why I brought you here. You must tell your daughter how it was, and she must tell her daughter. So it doesn't get lost, this part of the story: the way Jesus was with women, the way he felt we were real and important, and as wise as anyone. It's part of how he turned everything upside down.

The Red Egg

Legends do not grow up around inconsequential people. There are myths and legends that depict Mary Magdalene's ability to perform miracles. An adaptation of one told by a nun in the Cathedral of Mary Magdalene to Elisabeth Moltmann-Wendel is included here.

Eggs and butterflies are highly symbolic of new life and the capacity to give new birth. To this very day, if you visit the Mary Magdalene Cathedral in Jerusalem you will find a beautiful statue of Mary Magdalene holding a red egg.

I have often wondered why at Easter of 1985 a grandmother of the Russian Orthodox church in Leningrad gave me a red egg, decorated with gold butterflies, blue flowers, and flying angels. I have often wondered why we were all given red eggs on Easter morning in 1972, when an ecumenical group participated in Greek Orthodox liturgies in Crete.

Why red? This myth helped me understand why.

Red is understood by churches today as the color for victory or celebration. The colored egg has traditionally been associated with Astarte, goddess of spring, from whose name our "Easter" is derived. Colored eggs were used in the spring celebrations honoring the goddess. Today's Easter tradition of giving colored eggs has been adopted by the churches. The practice of giving red eggs has transformed the traditional myth with fresh meaning for Christians.

The Red Egg

Mary Magdalene was sure Jesus was alive. She was the first to speak to him after he had been raised from the dead. She had seen him. It happened in the garden.

He had called her by name, "Mary."

She had replied to him, "Rabboni. Master."

She ran off to tell the others the wonderful news. On her way she met one of the disciples and told him the wondrous news.

"Jesus is alive. He has risen," she shouted in joy.

"I don't believe you. Prove it," argued the disciple.

At that very moment a woman carrying a basket of eggs passed by and Mary took an egg in her hand. As she held it up before the disciple, the egg turned a brilliant red – the color of victory.

To this very day, many Christians around the world give each other red eggs at Easter, to remind each other of the risen Christ.

New Life
John 20:1–2,11–13

This legend of the Anishinabe native people was written by Elder Gladys Taylor, Curve Lake, Ontario, for the 1990 Lenten Booklet of the United Church of Canada and is used with permission. A native person, she takes the thread of her experience and deep spiritual connection to creation, along with her knowledge and love of God, and tells the Easter story in a way that it might happen in a northern native community. In a previous story, Elder Taylor wrote of a family camped for a long winter up north, and how they welcomed into their tipi a stranger who was not well dressed and who was very cold. They bedded him down, fed him, and felt his warmth as he spoke to them in his strange language. He held his drink in his cupped hands and they saw a "faint light around his head." They hoped he would stay with them, but when they awoke in the morning he was gone. For two days they followed his tracks. On the third day, they found where he had fallen and died. "In a short time you will no longer see me, and then a short time later you will see me again" (John 16:16–20).

The story "New Life" is inspired by John 20:1–2, 11–13 which tells of the empty tomb and resurrection. The close relationship between human beings, animals, and the natural world reflected in this story is also a familiar theme in theology out of women's struggles. "New Life" celebrates the joy in discovery of the many gifts left to the native people (brought to them?) by their new found "returned" friend. They perceive that the gifts are for the betterment of all people.

For Further Reading

Spirit of Gentleness, Lenten Readings and Prayers, Joyce Carlson ed., The United Church of Canada, 1988.

New Life

story by Gladys Taylor, Curve Lake, Ontario

On the third day they found where the stranger had fallen and died. Placing his body on a travois, they brought him back to camp. The women rushed out, believing the men to be returning from the hunt. When they discovered it was the stranger they had grown to love, they were so very sad.

Of the many ermine they had caught in the fall they made a beautiful blanket and wrapped his body. They took the body back to the place where he had died in the forest, to the place where he had fallen and his hair had frozen to the ground. After digging his grave and placing his body in it, they sang and smoked a peace pipe.

When the warmth of spring arrived, they said to each other, "Let's go to the grave." When they arrived they saw a small tree with black markings; they thought it was an ermine tree! It seemed they could almost see it growing. The grass that grew around it was a most beautiful grass with a wonderful and sweet smell. As they were there, enjoying the sweet smell, they seemed to hear a voice.

"I am going to give you a skill to be copied by many people, and this is the way you will teach them; you will fashion baskets from this special tree. I will send you an animal that will sacrifice his coat for the decoration of this basket, and for finishing the basket you will use the sweetgrass, the hair that has grown out of the earth."

And that is how the Anishinabe people learned to work with birchbark baskets. As they were watching and listening, they saw a little animal on the path. The animal was looking at them; as they looked the animal fell before them. And so it was that the animal gave its coat for the decoration of the basket and sweetgrass was used for the finishing of the basket.

Many people from different cultures have now learned this craft from us, the Anishinabe people of Canada. This is the way we learned about the making of baskets and we use it for the betterment of our people. We have received this from the Great Spirit.

Women's Initiative
(in the Exodus Stories)

The stories that follow deal with the Exodus of the Israelites from Egypt, the pivotal event in the Hebrew Scriptures. Before attempting to tell or read these stories to children, read the appropriate scripture for yourself from at least three Bible translations: New English Bible, New Revised Standard Version, or the Jerusalem Bible.

The book of Exodus begins with the list of names of the 12 sons of Jacob who went down to Egypt (verses 1–5). Over time, their offspring filled the land (verses 6–7). When a new Pharaoh came to power, the trouble started.

The well-known story of the Hebrews' struggle for deliverance from Egypt is told through selected stories that highlight the women who made Moses' leadership possible. The stories focus on the courageous and subtle disobedience of the midwives Puah and Shiphrah (Exodus 1:15–22); the resourcefulness of Moses' mother Jochabed (Exodus 2:1–10); the quick thinking sister Miriam (Exodus 2:1–10); the compassionate Egyptian Princess and her maids (Exodus 2:1–10); and the initiative of Moses' Midianite wife Zipporah (Exodus 4:18ff).

Pharaoh thought that Hebrew baby boys and men would be his undoing.

But it was the women! In the refusal of women to cooperate with oppression, the liberation of Israel from Egyptian bondage and the struggle for justice had its beginnings. The power of women is subtly hidden in the biblical text.

Traditional interpretation of the biblical stories focuses on Moses the future leader. What is usually not acknowledged is the creative contribution of the women, starting with the civil disobedience of the midwives, and ending with Zipporah, a foreign woman, fitting Moses for leadership by insisting on his circumcision.

A cursory look at the contemporary ecumenical world-wide scene reveals an awareness of the Exodus as God's "No" to exploitation. The meaning Israel found in the Exodus event has been appropriated by those in similar situations of economic, socio-political or racist exploitation.

At Christmas, 1987, the offices of the Christian Conference of Asia were forcibly closed by the Singapore Government, the files seized, the financial assets frozen, and the staff deported to other Asian countries. The government defended its actions by claiming that the Christian churches which were part of the Conference were communist. This was by virtue of the fact that they worked to organize the poor for a better economic future. Asia teems with the poor. Christians saw their mission to stand with the poor and exploited. They read the Exodus event as God's definitive "No" to the powerful Pharaohs of this world who specialize in exploitation of people. You will find some of this experience reflected in the story "Pharaoh's Daughter," adapted from a dramatization of Exodus 1–2 by theologian Rev. Sun Ai Park, one of those deported from Singapore.

Liberation theology in Latin America draws much of its biblical foundation from the Exodus story. The deliverance of the Hebrews from economic servitude is, for the 80 per cent of Latin Americans who are desperately poor, a paradigm of God's just and compassionate intention in history.

South African theologians echo the same ideas. Desmond Tutu's favorite text is, "Let my people go!" At the World Council of Churches' Vancouver 1983 meeting, Tutu waved a Bible on high and shouted, "When your missionaries brought us this book, telling of the prophets all tied up with kings and exploitation, did they not know we would take it seriously?"

South African black theologian Itumeleng Mosala writes, "To participate in the struggles of the texts [of the Bible] empowers people to participate in the struggles of contemporary communities of faith. The Bible is the product, the record, the site, and the weapon of class, cultural, gender and racial struggles. To these struggles the Exodus event is central." (Itumeleng J. Mosala, *Biblical Hermeneutics and Black Theology in South Africa*, Grand Rapids: Wm. B. Eerdmans,1988, p. 193.)

A Hard Choice

Traditionally, the stories in Exodus 1 and 2 focus on Moses. Rarely do commentaries mention the courageous role of the midwives Puah and Shiphrah. Yet they are instrumental in saving the child who became Israel's deliverer. The Bible identifies them as Hebrew women. Yet they have Egyptian names. Elsa Tamez, a Central American theologian, thinks that they were probably Egyptians, for who else would Pharaoh trust with executing his orders? Others say they were Hebrews, but with names common in Egyptian culture.

In any case, these two women could have chosen a normal, quiet, safe life. Instead, they joined the freedom struggles of the Israelites. With these women's affirmation of life, their subversion of injustice, and their civil disobedience, movements for liberation began long before Moses appeared on the scene.

Ordinary women chose to disobey a cruel and unjust law involving the destruction of life. They feared God more than man. Through their daring action, many lives were saved, including that of the one who was eventually to deliver their nation. It has been part of women's upbringing, in most cultures, to be obedient and submissive, and to put up with injustice, cruelty, and death itself as "women's lot." Stories like this remind us that there is a time when we must not submit, nor even merely observe, but must actively resist injustice to ourselves and to others. (Reading the Bible as Asian Women, *Christian Conference of Asia, Singapore, p. 66.)*

You've heard the story of Moses and the bulrushes. Here is a story that goes with it.

As a storyteller you might want to draw the parallel with the Greek scripture's account of Herod and his slaughter of the baby boys. Such a comparison would prevent us from seeing a split between the Greek and Hebrew scriptures. They do, after all, address the same themes.

For Further Reading

Exum, Cheryl J. "You Shall Let Every Daughter Live." *Semeia*, Atlanta: Scholars Press, p. 64.

A Hard Choice

This poem is with apologies to
A. A. Milne's Christopher Robin.

Hebrew midwives, Puah and Shiphrah,
Said to themselves, said they
"Is Pharaoh trying to destroy us
When to Hebrew boys he says, 'Nay.'"

Puah and Shiphrah, known as the midwives,
Decided to outwit the King.
Puah and Shiphrah found a good way
For Pharaoh to have his last fling.

Puah and Shiphrah, told Pharaoh
"Pharaoh" they said, said they.
"Hebrew mothers, faster than others,
Deliver their babies quick-e-lay."

Puah and Shiphrah told the people,
"People" said Puah, said she,
"Nobody oughter throw babes in the water
If they don't want to tangle with me!"

There were once two wise women, Puah and Shiphrah. They were called "midwives." They helped mothers who were going to have a baby.

Puah's name meant "Splendor" and Shiphrah's meant "Beauty." Despite their names, they were not dressed in splendor, nor did they look like beauties. They were very poor. They did not have splendid clothes. They seldom had enough to eat. They had neither sandals nor shoes.

These two wise women were ordered to come before the Pharaoh (the title given to the King of Egypt) in his palace. When Puah and Shiphrah entered the throne room Pharaoh was sitting on his splendid throne of gold and sapphires. The room was very big. It had high ceilings and rich carpets.

Puah and Shiphrah felt as small as grasshoppers. They had never before been in the presence of a rich and powerful Pharaoh. They were very frightened.

Now Pharaoh thought there were too many Hebrews in the land of Egypt. They were as many as the grains of sand on a beach. Pharaoh was afraid they would fight against him. They might even try to kick him off his throne!

So he made them slaves. He had no pity on them. He made cruel rules. He made them work hard from morning until night. They made bricks to build his cities. They worked in the blazing sun. They planted his fields. They were very poor. Pharaoh was very rich.

Yet the Hebrews had many babies. Pharaoh knew he had to put a stop to this. So he gave an order to Puah and Shiphrah.

"When you help a Hebrew woman give birth to a baby, keep your eye on the child. If it's a boy, kill him. If it's a girl, who cares?" he thundered.

Puah and Shiphrah could not believe their ears.

"What a wicked law," raged Shiphrah to herself.

But they could say nothing. They bowed low before the mighty Pharaoh, backed out of the glittering throne room, and left the palace.

"How dare the Pharaoh order all the baby boys killed," raved Puah. "Doesn't he know they are people too? Why are women punished for having baby boys?"

"God wants babies to live, not die," said Shiphrah.

The midwives had learned to fear God more than to fear Pharaoh. So they thought about letting the boys live.

"But if we don't obey Pharaoh what will happen to us?" worried Puah. "Will he kill us if we don't obey his law?"

"I don't know," confided Shiphrah fearfully. "We have to make a hard choice. Obey Pharaoh and do what we believe is wrong? Or save the baby boys and take the punishment Pharaoh will give us?"

They decided not to obey Pharaoh. They would save the baby boys.

Pharaoh was puzzled. The number of Hebrews grew larger, not smaller. For the second time, he sent for the two midwives. They didn't dare look up at him.

"What are you up to?" he thundered from his high throne of gold and sapphires. He acted as though he were a mighty eagle and they were only small hummingbirds. "Why are you letting the baby boys live?"

"Oh great Pharaoh," said Shiphrah, her head down and her eyes fixed on Pharaoh's feet, "the Hebrew women are not like Egyptian women. They are strong and lively. They give birth to babies easily and quickly."

"Yes," echoed Puah. "Their babies are born before we arrive. We don't even know whether a boy or a girl has been born."

Pharaoh was so angry that he wanted to jump up and down and scream, or pull out his beard hair by hair. But he was a king. So instead, he thought to himself, "I must put a final stop to this."

Puah and Shiphrah bowed low and left the palace. Safe outside the palace gates, they looked at each other.

"Do you think he really believed our story?" asked Shiphrah.

"I think he did," laughed Puah as she winked at Shiphrah. "Besides, it's true what we said. Hebrew women do give birth to their babies more quickly than Egyptian women do."

"He is a wicked, wicked king. He knows nothing of a God who wants babies to live," said Shiphrah.

"So why shouldn't he believe us?" asked Puah.

They joined hands and whirled in a circle for joy at what had happened. Their laughter echoed off the nearby hills. God blessed the midwives and gave them children of their own. And the Hebrews continued to grow in numbers and became as many as the stars in the sky.

Then Pharaoh made another stronger rule. He ordered all the people to obey it. "Throw every newborn Hebrew boy into the Nile River. Who cares about girls."

Puah and Shiphrah thought, "He doesn't care about us either."

"Everybody will be watching the Hebrew women to see if the baby is a boy or a girl," Puah said. "What will happen? Will baby boys be drowned in the River Nile? Will there be a way to save them?"

It wasn't for nothing the midwives' names meant "Splendor" and "Beauty." For then Shiphrah said a perfectly beautiful and splendid thing.

"Don't worry Puah," she said in a quiet even voice. "We love God and so do not obey the wicked Pharaoh. There will be a way for God's justice to win. We will find it."

Miriam's Story

At least six obedient women saved Moses' life: Puah and Shiphrah, the midwives who practiced civil disobedience; his older sister Miriam; his mother Jochabed, who gave up her son so he would survive; the Pharaoh's daughter, who resisted the injustice of her father's decree; and Zipporah, Moses' "foreign" spouse, who understood the importance of his being circumcised, and acted appropriately.

Their plan won, and God won through them. There is irony in that the mighty Pharaoh's schemes for death are undermined by women with a commitment to human life and dignity.

The story ends with the Princess' naming of the baby. She calls him Moses, which means "the one drawn out." The Hebrew verb is more accurately translated actively as "the drawer out." The name points to Moses' future life, when he became in a special way, the "drawer out" of the Hebrews from slavery in Egypt.

At this main turning point in biblical history, Miriam plays a key role. Significantly, the root meaning of the name Miriam is "rebel." Here is her story.

Miriam's Story

A Pat-a-Cake Game

The first two lines of each "verse" should be said in a singsong voice and in rhythm to the accompaniment of four hand claps. The child's part is the "no no" line, to four claps.

Who saved the baby boys
from Pha-raoh?
Who let the Hebrew boys live?
(clap)

Who helped the Princess
at the waa-ter?
Who fetched the basket for her?
(clap)

Abraham?
No no no no. Puah did.

Joseph?
No no no no. Her maid did.

Who thought to make a
little bas-ket?
Who put the basket in the ree-eeds?

Who took the baby to the paa-lace?
Who brought him up as her own?
(clap)

Isaac?
No no no no. Miriam did.

Pharaoh?
No no no no. The Princess did.

Who nursed the baby with
her own milk?
Who loved him but gave him up?
(clap)

Jacob?
No no no no. Jochabed did.

Miriam's Story

story by Rose Ferries, Winnipeg

Miriam scuffed at a small stone as she followed her mother to the river bank. Things had changed so much in the past few months. She used to be the baby of the family. Her mother used to have lots of time to brush her long hair, to teach her to sew and to bake bread. But then that baby brother arrived. Little Seth.
He cried.

He fussed.

He got hungry.

He needed changing.

And her mother was always worried about hiding him because of the Pharaoh. The Pharaoh wanted his soldiers to kill all the Hebrew baby boys.

So Miriam's mother never had time for her any more. Miriam had to brush her own hair. She had to try to sew a dress for her doll all by herself. And when she wanted to bake with her mother, her mother always said, "Miriam, go and watch over Seth and see that he doesn't cry." Miriam wished things could be the way they used to be. Before the baby.

Seth grew bigger and bigger. And his crying got louder. One day, Seth cried all morning long. Mother was afraid that someone would hear him and report him. So she took the baby and put him in a basket made of tightly-woven bulrushes. It was the basket Miriam used for her dolls but her mother said she'd get her another one soon. Miriam did as her mother asked. She tucked Seth into the basket and set it at the edge of the river. You could hardly see it for the reeds. Then Miriam sat down to see what would happen.

She was amazed. Seth stopped crying. He just lay in his little

basket and watched the birds. He had a cute toothless smile. Maybe
he wasn't such a nuisance after all.

Suddenly Miriam heard laughter. It was the Egyptian Princess
and her maids coming down to the river. Miriam was afraid. What
would happen if the Princess saw Seth?

"Ssshh" she whispered to Seth. "Keep still and maybe she
won't notice you. If she does, we're all in big trouble."

But just then, Seth began to cry, a loud wail that no one could
mistake for anything but a baby! The Princess heard the sound
and whirled around in surprise. She thought they were alone at
the river. They looked in the direction of the cry. The Princess
spied the baby in the basket and sent one of her maids to bring
him to her.

"Oh, isn't he sweet" they all cooed. "He has such bright eyes
and so much dark hair."

The Egyptian Princess made a decision. "This is one of the
Hebrew children. We can't just leave him here in the river where he
might drown. I am going to take him home and keep him and he
can live with me."

From her hiding place, Miriam listened to everything the
women said. They were going to take her little brother away! To her
surprise she realized that she would miss him. When he had smiled
earlier that afternoon he had looked right at her. Besides, he was
only a baby and he would be scared without anyone from his family.

Miriam got an idea. She ran up to the Princess and said, "I know
someone who can nurse your baby for you. Shall I go find her?"

The Princess, who didn't know much about looking after babies, thought it was a splendid idea. So Miriam ran off as fast as she
could to get her mother. Maybe she would get to keep her baby
brother for a while after all.

■■■■■

The Pharaoh's Daughter
Exodus 2:1–10

There are many ways to interpret the story known as Moses in the bulrushes (Exodus 2:1–10). The Egyptian daughter of Pharaoh is the focus of our story. In her role as lead player she provides several surprises. There is a wonderful phrase she uses when she says to Moses' mother, "Take this child and nurse him for me. I will see you are paid," (Exodus 2:9). What an extraordinary thing for an Egyptian to say to a sworn enemy, a helpless Hebrew. This same saying is echoed in the Greek scriptures. The Good Samaritan says to the innkeeper in Jesus' parable, "Take care of him (the helpless Jewish victim) and on my way back I will make good any extra expenses you have," (Luke 10:35). The Pharaoh's daughter does exactly what the Good Samaritan did for the innocent victim. These words from Exodus may have been in Jesus' mind when he told the parable.

The story underlines the necessity of demonstrating God's grace and generosity to one who is not only an enemy, but also of a different race, culture and religion. The Pharaoh's daughter, a woman of color, of Egyptian culture, and of the faith of Isis, reaches across barriers of race, religion, culture, and gender to include the stranger Moses. What a contemporary lesson that could be for our children! That is why we include it along with "Getting Even" a contemporary story of generosity across barriers of hate.

The roles of the three maids are adapted from a drama written by Rev. Sun Ai Park of South Korea. The three maids are symbolic of three attitudes open to Asian women in such tense times.

- Don't trust anybody, particularly foreigners or people of different color or faith. Women will get the worst of it if they disobey their "own" people.
- Adopt a pessimistic attitude and try to be apolitical. Politics are not for women. This really involves "supporting the status quo."
- Always be curious and hopeful. Commit yourself to justice.

The Pharaoh's Daughter

adapted from a drama written by
Rev. Sun Ai Park, South Korea

(Here are some finger plays. Make up your own actions.)

Here is Moses   *Here is Miriam*
Afloat in the water   *Hid with her mother*
Waiting around   *Courageously daring,*
For Pharaoh's daughter   *Saving her brother*

"It's so-o-o hot," said the Pharaoh's daughter. She took off her red sandals, admired her red painted toenails, and wriggled her toes in the cool white sand. It was a beautiful and peaceful morning.

"I can hardly wait to get into the cool water and wash the sweat and dust off myself," she mused.

The wind played in the bulrushes. Small waves from the river lapped the shore, and the sun shone brilliantly.

Just as she was dipping one toe into the water, her first maid-in-waiting, who was usually down-in-the-mouth, said, "Be careful Princess. Look, there is something stuck in the bulrushes. I can't tell from here what it is, but it's probably some garbage that will pollute your bathing spot."

"Listen," said the second maid, who was usually suspicious, "I hear something that sounds like a whimper. Do you hear it? Do you think it's an animal?"

"I see it. It's just a basket," said the third maid, who was usually curious and hopeful. "And look – the lid has breathing holes in it. I wonder what it could be? Let's find out."

"Fetch me the basket," ordered the Pharaoh's daughter.

The small whimper had turned into a great howl. The maid who was usually curious and hopeful fetched the basket and then hurried to give it to the Pharaoh's daughter. She opened the lid of the basket. Inside was a baby howling its lungs out. Its face was squished up and red with the effort.

"Why it's – it's a baby!" squealed the Pharaoh's daughter with delight. "Look how big its hands are. And what a beautifully shaped head. I wish I had such a baby."

"It must be one of the Hebrew baby boys," suggested the maid who was usually down-in-the-mouth. "If he is, he hasn't much of a life ahead of him. Throw him back into the river as your father ordered."

"Don't have anything to do with that basket, Princess," said the second maid. "We have no idea who put the baby there. Maybe it's a trap. Leave the baby in its little ark, I say. Rescuing babies is not up to you."

"Let's at least have a look," urged the third maid. She lifted the baby out of the basket and placed him in the arms of Pharaoh's daughter.

"Isn't he beautiful?" exclaimed Pharaoh's daughter. "Look, there's a little gas pain that made him smile. I think it's terrible that a mother should have to hide her baby," she said. She stamped her foot and frowned. "My father should never have ordered the killing of all Hebrew baby boys. I think I will save this one."

"Princess," said the first maid who was by this time extremely down-in-the-mouth, "you shouldn't interfere with your father's affairs – whether they are just or unjust, whether they make people happy or sad. That is the business of men, not women like you."

"I know my father will be angry if I disobey him. But I'm angry with him! This order is making too many people unhappy," said the Princess.

At that moment, a small girl who had been hiding in the rushes took a risk and stepped forward.

"I know a woman who has plenty of milk who could be the wet nurse to this baby," she said hesitantly.

"Be careful Princess," said the second maid. "She looks like a Hebrew to me. They are your enemies. After all, this baby is probably a Hebrew too, and not of your race. And the baby's family probably doesn't worship the goddess Isis as you do."

"Hebrew milk won't be as good for the baby as Egyptian milk," warned the first maid.

"None of that makes any difference does it?" asked the third maid. "He's a human being. You have a chance to save a life, Princess."

The Pharaoh's daughter took the risk.

"I am going to care for this baby," she said. Then she turned to the small girl. "Go and fetch the wet nurse you mentioned. I will pay her. When the baby is grown big enough to be weaned, bring him to me in the palace and I will raise him as my own."

"May the God of Justice give you a long life," exclaimed the baby's real mother, when the little girl had brought her from her hiding place in the bulrushes nearby. The baby's real mother was the wet nurse the little girl had meant all along.

The Princess gave the baby to the third maid to hold.

"Come. Rejoice with me," said the Pharaoh's daughter, to her two other maids. "I have saved a life! For once in our lives, let all the women celebrate together." Then she gave the baby back to her mother.

The baby's mother, and little girl whose name was Miriam, watched as the Princess and her maids left the sandy beach and returned to the palace. Then they offered a prayer of thanks to God for saving the life of the Hebrew baby.

Getting Even

This story of a Pacific Island king has the same theme of generosity to one's enemies. It is a story from the churches of Micronesia, written by Alice Buck and adapted from the Pacific Islands Christian Education Curriculum (Youth First Year, 1966).

It comes to us through the United Church of Christ. Its setting is World War II and the soldiers referred to are Japanese. King John Sigrah of Kosrae was a Christian minister as well as king.

This story is for older children.

Getting Even

adapted from a story
by Alice Buck

Many years ago, there was a king called John Sigrah. He was king of a small island called Kosrae. It was surrounded by the mighty Pacific Ocean.

One day, strangers came to the island. They were soldiers. They shot their guns at the people and killed ten men. They took 20 others as captives. They said there was a war, and that the islanders were their enemies. They ordered all the men to build barricades and dig ditches in which the soldiers could hide should there be an attack on the island. Even the women and the children were ordered to work for the soldiers. They had to carry heavy pails of water and were not given enough to eat.

King John told his people that they were not to work for the soldiers. He told them they were not slaves. They were not to take orders from the strangers who had taken over their island.

The soldiers took King John and tortured him. They burnt his skin with lighted cigarettes.

The men of Kosrae refused to work for their enemies who treated them so cruelly.

The women of Kosrae refused to work for their enemies who treated them so cruelly.

The children of Kosrae refused to work for their enemies who treated them so cruelly.

The commander of the soldiers pushed tiny slivers of bamboo beneath the king's fingernails. Still the people of Kosrae refused to work for their enemies who treated them so cruelly.

When the war was over the soldiers left the island and another visitor arrived. She wanted to hear how the people of the island had fared during the war.

"I heard the enemy soldiers treated you very cruelly during the war," the visitor said to the king.

King John nodded. "Yes, they did," he admitted. Then he added quickly, "But I got even with them."

The visitor was astonished to hear the king say this. The king was known for his generosity and kindness. He was not known to have ever taken revenge on anyone.

"What did you do?" the visitor asked curiously.

King John smiled. "When the soldiers were hungry, I took them food!"

A Pair of Sealskin Boots

"By faith, Moses, when he grew up, refused to be called the son of Pharaoh's daughter, preferring to suffer hardship with the people of God," (Hebrews 11:24, N.E.B.).

A few years ago, I spent an afternoon in Winnipeg talking with three native women – Nanette McKay, Mary David, and Virginia Smith. I asked them how they would tell the Moses in the bulrushes story to their children or grandchildren. They said there were three questions they would like to have answered before they put the story together.

First, how did Moses really feel about being adopted out to a strange family, country, culture, religion, race?

Second, how was he able to establish his Hebrew identity?

Third, what prompted him to assume leadership for his people? Why didn't he just assimilate into Egypt?

Moses' story is our story, the native women told me – one of adoption, lost identity, and assumption of leadership.

It took me some time to locate a contemporary woman whose story parallels that of Moses in those three respects. Her name is Sue Anderson now, and she lives on the Rama reserve in Ontario. She was born Inuit, with the name Sue Nakalook. She was adopted into an Anglo-Saxon family after a tragic accident. With the support of her adoptive family and with help from others she established her own identity and early roots. It took 42 years to do so. She married a native Indian, and now is listed by the Canadian Government as "Indian." As she began to share the problems and the life of Indian people in Canada, she found herself catapulted into a leadership position within the native community. This woman, who has bridged three cultures, told a small part of her astonishing story to me.

A Pair of Sealskin Boots

My name was Sue Nakalook. Until I was about six years old, I lived with my family on an island in the far north of Canada. My people were called Inuit. There was lots of snow and I loved to play games with my brothers and sisters. There were a few white men around – men in the army and navy who sent weather pictures down south, or who watched for enemy submarines under the ice. It was during the war.

One day, when we were playing around a fire ringed with rocks, I accidentally tripped and fell into the fire. I don't remember what happened next. I was told it all later, when I grew up.

My cousin Mark pulled me out. I was put on a plane and flown down south to a hospital in The Pas, Manitoba. One of the army men who flew with me in the plane told me that he couldn't see anything of me except my eyes. I had so many bandages. All of my body from the neck down was badly burned. My fingers were fused together so my hand looked like the webbed foot of a duck. I don't remember this, but it's what I was told later. My sister, who is six years older than I am, came and stayed with me for three months. She didn't speak English, nor did I. We spoke the Inuit language. I was in the hospital there for a year and a half.

I didn't see anyone of my family again for 42 years.

There was a white couple living in The Pas named Margaret and Ken who could not have children of their own. Margaret wanted a child badly. She heard about me from her doctor who suggested she visit me. She did, for all of that year and a half. She was a school teacher, and began to teach me things. She sang to me. I learned "Jesus loves me," from her and thought I could speak English because I could sing it! Everything was so strange. They wanted to adopt me right then, but the government stepped in and put me into orphanages, residential schools and foster homes until I was 18 years old. It was all a blur of people and places I didn't know. Everything was strange to me. I had never been off my island before.

Margaret and Ken had a lot of struggle with the government about adopting me. Finally they won, and I went to live with them. They loved me, and I loved them. I trained as a nurse.

All that time I wondered about my Inuit family. Margaret and Ken knew I had come from "the north" but they were not allowed to look at government records. The records listed a number for every Inuit person, but we never got to see what my number was. If we had, we might have traced my Inuit family. I longed to see and know them. The two men who had flown me to The Pas hospital, one in the army and one in the navy, never stopped trying to locate my family. They had a hard time, because the government had moved all my people to another island farther north.

One day, after I grew up, I went to an Inuit art show in Ontario. The man in charge was interested that I was Inuit. He phoned a friend of his who lived up north to look in the computer for the name "Nakalook." I had a phone call from the man in the north.

"Are you sitting down?" he asked. "You have a loving family up here, a huge family." He gave me my Inuit number that was re-corded in government records. Then he gave me the number of my sister Annie (who was listed one ahead of me) and of my brother (who was listed one behind me). "You have parents, grandparents, lots and lots of relatives. You belong to a huge family," he said.

I burst into tears. It was the first I knew who I was. "Your grandparents have kept your story alive in the north," he said.

"They never gave up hope of finding you, but didn't know how to do that." Later, I found out that my Inuit grandparents always had a healing circle and prayed for me. My grandfather wouldn't move to the new island when the government moved my people, because he thought I might come back and find nobody there any more. Eight men had to put him on the plane when they finally moved him.

I paid a six week visit to my Inuit family, arriving on June 28, 1989. They called that day "Susie's Day." For four days we just cried. It was so wonderful to know them all. But it was terrible what the government had done all those years by keeping us apart. I was sick and sad because of that.

Hardly anybody spoke English, and I couldn't speak the Inuit language. I would say a sentence. Then it would have to be said in the Inuit language. Then my sister or a member of the family would say a sentence in the Inuit language. Then it would have to be repeated in English so I could understand. It took hours and hours, but it was worth it. They treated me like a ghost – feeling my arms and legs to reassure themselves that I really did exist. They had heard my story so many times. Here I was finally, in the flesh.

We feasted and danced from noon until four the next morning. What gifts they gave me! My sister made me a pair of sealskin boots – kamicks they call them. They were knee high, with small stitching. My nephew had shot the seal, and my sister taught me how to clean it and prepare the skin for winter boots. It took one week to sew one boot! My cousin gave me a beautiful ivory ring he had carved, with an ivory seal on it for decoration.

When I flew south, Margaret and Ken met me. "What's it like finding your own family," they asked. I knew I was Inuit. But I was also their daughter. "No," I said. "I found my extended family. You are my mother and father."

Some years before, I had married an Indian native man, an

Ojibwa, and gone to live with him on the Rama Indian reserve. In the eyes of the government, this made me an Indian! They listed my name in the Indian Band records and gave me a number. My Certificate of Indian status lists me as "Sue Anderson" since that is now my name. I entered a world I didn't know anything about. I began to understand the problems native Indian people have in Canada.

I had purchased a house before I married and "became an Indian." Now the government, who considered me "Indian" told me that I couldn't buy property that was not on the Indian reserve. It was against the law for Indians to do so. Anybody coming to settle in Canada can do so. But not Indians. I began to work for justice for Indian people. I knew what it was to live off the Indian reserve. I also knew what it was to live on it. The elders of my reserve noticed me working away at justice for people, and called me to be a leader. They promised to help me. Ever since I've been working for justice for people.

I couldn't do it without the love of those two men who saved my life by flying me to The Pas. I couldn't do it without the love of my husband, and of my mother Margaret, and my father Ken. I couldn't do it without knowing I have the support of a big Inuit family, still living their lives in the far north of Canada.

The Mark of Belonging
Exodus 4:18

After killing an Egyptian, Moses fled Egypt and lived in Midian, a foreign country. He married Zipporah, a Midianite and a foreigner, and she bore him their first child, a son named Gershom. God called Moses to return to Egypt and lead his people out of bondage. But Moses resisted: he thought he would face criminal charges; he had been raised in the Egyptian court and might not be accepted by his own people; and he knew he didn't speak well. Above all, he had not been circumcised. Yet now he was returning as though he were a Hebrew.

At the time this story was written, circumcision was an essential mark of being Hebrew. It was the mark of belonging, similar to baptism as the mark of belonging for a Christian. But who would circumcise him? The Midianites in whose land he lived, could not do it as they themselves were not circumcised. Vicariously, Moses' son Gershom, the son of a Hebrew father (which in those days *made* him a Hebrew), accomplished the circumcision through Zipporah's intervention. Exodus 4:25–26 tells the story. Zipporah first circumcised

their young son Gershom. "She cut off her son's foreskin and touched Moses' feet with it." The Hebrew word for "feet" here is used to refer to the genitals. Her act was understood as being the same as circumcising Moses.

Usually the story focuses on Moses. Women focus on Zipporah, who made Moses fit for leadership. Her role is not widely known, yet it is pivotal in Moses' ability to accomplish his leadership role as a Hebrew. Although a foreigner, Zipporah understood the requirements and power of Moses' God Yahweh even *before* the Exodus.

Moses must be circumcised. Verse 24 says, "The Lord met Moses, meaning to kill him." Why, if God had just called him to return to Egypt to lead his people, would God want to kill him? It was because he was not circumcised, not marked as an authentic Hebrew man. Yet verse 26 says, "The Lord let Moses alone." Having now received the mark of belonging from Zipporah, God accepted him as a fit leader for the people.

Thus we begin to understand Zipporah's vital role. She knew all of this before Moses did, and she acted decisively. She acted on faith, not waiting for a demonstration of Yahweh's power. Her initiative made a significant contribution to the success of the Exodus. She is a strong role model for girls and women.

The three stories, "The Mark of Belonging," "Sunday School," and "My First Trip" should be read in sequence. The first one emphasizes Christian baptism as the "sign of belonging" for Christians. The second and third stories highlight circumcision as the "sign of belonging" for the Israelites.

The Mark of Belonging

inspired by a sermon
by Rev. Stan Lucyk

I was having lunch with my dad at a restaurant after church one Sunday.

"I'd like fries and a burger," I said.

"We may have to wait a bit," my dad replied. "That young man is the only waiter on duty today. But he's quick."

Sure enough, the waiter soon came to our table.

"Thank you for being so prompt," Dad said.

The owner must have heard him because he came over to our

table. He put his arm around the young waiter and said, "He's a good waiter. He arrived recently from Egypt." The waiter, now grinning broadly at his boss's kind words, hurried off to get my fries and burger.

When he came back to our table he noticed the small cross I wore around my neck. He rolled up his sleeve and showed me his bare arm. He had a tattoo of a cross just above his wrist.

"I was tattooed with the sign of the cross at my baptism," he said. "That's the way we do it in our church in Egypt."

"That's the same sign the minister made in church. She made it on my baby sister's forehead. First she poured some water on Laura's head and then made the sign on Laura's forehead with her fingers," I said.

"That's right Julie," Dad said. "She baptized Laura with the sign of the cross. When you were baptized the same thing happened to you. It means that both Laura and you bear the mark of belonging to the Christian family."

"But doesn't she belong to our family?"

"Of course she does. We love her dearly. But she also belongs to the Christian family. So do you and so do I."

"I do too," the waiter emphasized, pointing to his tattoo. "You are my friends."

We knew we all belonged together.

Sunday School

One Sunday, Julie raced home from Sunday school. She could hardly wait to tell her dad what she had heard.

"It was a story about Moses. But it reminded me of the Egyptian waiter. But there was no water like there was with baby Laura's baptism." Her words gushed out in a torrent.

"Julie, Julie, slow down. What is it?" asked her dad.

"It was our Bible story at Sunday school. It was about a brave woman and what she did. She gave Moses the mark of belonging, just like the minister gave Laura the mark of belonging. The woman had a long name. I can't remember it."

"You must mean Zipporah. She was Moses' wife, but she was an outsider, a foreigner."

"Yes she was, but that didn't make any difference. She knew God wanted it and that Moses must have the mark of belonging. So she did it."

"Did what?"

"Gave him the mark of belonging. The teacher said it was called the covenant. I can't remember the long name for it."

"It is called circumcision."

"Yes, that's it. It was very important to Moses and to the people of Israel to know they belonged together. And the woman was the one who did it. I think God smiled."

My First Trip
Exodus 4:18–26, 18:1–12

Our story begins with Moses' circumcision (the removal of the foreskin of the penis as a religious ritual, a sign of the covenant, and of belonging to the people of Israel) through the eyes of Gershom, his son. Then it moves on. After the Israelites' Exodus from Egypt, Moses returns to Midian to his wife Zipporah and his family, and to his father-in-law Jethro. The men retire almost immediately to a tent to talk of "all the Lord had done to Pharaoh and to Egypt for Israel's sake, and about their hardships on the journey, and how the Lord had saved them." Jethro expresses admiration for Moses' God and brings whole offerings and sacrifices to that God. And "Aaron and all the elders of Israel came and shared their meal with Jethro" (Exodus 18:8–12).

Fine, except where was Zipporah, the author of this great new story of Moses' mission? While the story tells of the men discussing all these marvelous public events, Zipporah is written out of the story. She, a foreign woman who courageously circumcised Moses in an act of faith, is ignored. Zipporah's experience is shared by many women today.

For Further Reading

Laffey, Alice L. "Zipporah – A First Ruth?" In *An Introduction to the Old Testament – A Feminist Perspective*, Philadelphia: Fortress, 1988.

My First Trip

Zipporah was from Midian
And she was Moses' wife,
She took the future in her hands
And then she saved his life.

Gershom never tired of hearing the story of his very first trip.

"You made your very first trip on the back of a donkey," said his mother Zipporah.

"What was the donkey's name?" asked Gershom.

"I called the donkey Josh. You were a baby and I carried you in my arms. I sang to match the donkey's hoofbeats:

'Clip clop, clip clop

Back to Egypt,

Then we'll stop.'"

"We had lived with your Grandpa Jethro in my country Midian since you were born. Your first trip was from Midian to Egypt."

"Why were we going to Egypt? Wasn't it nice in Midian?" Gershom asked.

"It was nice in Midian. But your father Moses is an Israelite. He didn't really *want* to live in Midian; he had just been hiding there. Years before you were born he had killed an Egyptian man who was being cruel to the Israelite slaves in Egypt. If the Egyptians had caught your father they would have killed him. So he left and hid in Midian. But then God told him to go back to Egypt. God wanted him to lead the Israelite people out of slavery. So we had to go back.

"It was hot and dusty," Zipporah continued. "We stopped for

the night. I couldn't sleep, even though I was very tired."

"Were scary night noises keeping you awake?"

"No. I like the night noises. I couldn't sleep because your father kept me awake. He told me he was sure that God would kill him before he got back to Egypt. I was terrified."

"Why would God do that?" asked Gershom.

Gershom's father, Zipporah explained, wasn't sure. But she knew. Gershom's father did not bear the mark of belonging to the family of Israel. She knew it was hard for Gershom to understand. But the mark of belonging was very important. Neither Gershom nor his father had been circumcised. That's the ceremony that made them part of the Israelite people.

"But God didn't kill him did he?" asked Gershom.

"No, because I gave both of you the mark of the family of Israel that very night," Zipporah said.

"Why hadn't we become true Israelites before? Then God wouldn't have been mad at father."

"Well, we had been living in my country Midian and nobody there could perform the ceremony. Unless it was done, the Israelite slaves in Egypt would think that your father was an outsider. They wouldn't trust him to lead them into freedom."

"Why did you do it?"

"I love you and your father. I decided then and there that I would do the ceremony for both of you. You would both be true sons of Israel."

"You'd do it, even though you were from Midian?"

"Yes, even though I'm not an Israelite. But I did it. It was the only way I could keep your father alive so he could free his people."

"Are you circumcised?"

"No. Only the men bear the mark of the family in just that way."

"And then what happened?"

"God liked what I did. God smiled. We got to Egypt safely but it was very dangerous for us there. The Egyptians thought we were a true Israelite family. They tried to make life very difficult for us. So your father sent us back to Midian. Then he joined us there after he led his people out of slavery."

"And that's the first time he saw my little brother Eliezer, right?"

"Right," said Zipporah. "It was wonderful to have your father back again. We didn't see much of him for a while though. He disappeared into Grandpa Jethro's tent, and they talked and talked far into the night."

"I remember that. I wanted him to play with me, but he was too busy. They were too busy to talk with you too, weren't they?"

"You remember that, do you? It's true. I was upset. After all, it was due to me that your father was recognized as an Israelite. To hear the men tell it, it was all their idea!"

"But I know what you did mother. And all because of my first trip," exclaimed Gershom.

The Waters of Life
Exodus 13:17–18; 14; 15:1–21

The pivotal event in the liberation of the Israelites was the Exodus. This story is about the crossing of the Red Sea, an event that delivered the Israelites from Egyptian slavery. They look to this event, even today, as the foundation of their existence as a nation and as a people.

Miriam's role was central to this story. Above all others, she was accorded the status of prophetess. It was Miriam who led the Hebrew women with timbrel and song, acts recognized as signs of prophetic power.

She was always closely associated with water, from the saving waters of the Nile river to the crossing of the Red Sea. In the desert, Miriam knew where to find wellsprings of living water for the people. When she died there was a drought on the land (Numbers 20:1–2). This story emphasizes the saving properties of water, which were symbolic of new life and new beginnings. That is partly why water is used in Christian baptism.

Rabbinic sources say that when the first Hebrew foot touched the Red Sea the waters parted and there was a dry path. I have incorporated that tradition and made Miriam the one to take that first step.

Don't get hung up on searching for a logical explanation for the parting of the Red Sea. Remember that, in the Judaic-Christian religion, the symbols which represent our quest for freedom, deliverance, and wholeness continue to be "crossing over a sea," "escaping a storm for safe haven," and moving from "chaos to order."

The text makes it appear as though Moses was the first to sing the song of victory (Exodus 15:1ff). Many words were added to the original terse text that Miriam sang, which appears in Exodus 15:21. However, tradition has it that Miriam led the victory song. This small fraction of the original song is one of the oldest parts of sacred scripture. It probably dates back to the twelfth century BCE.

The Waters of Life

Here is Miriam,
Here is the sea,
Here is the path,
See Israelites free!

"Miriam, get up," cried Aaron her brother. "The Egyptians are coming. Pharaoh has sent 600 horses and chariots after us. His warriors will be here by nightfall. I don't want to be a slave again. Get up Miriam. Get up. Move."

Miriam had dropped to the ground, exhausted. She was so tired. She and the others had been walking steadily since they left Egypt. A pillar of cloud by day and a pillar of fire by night had guided them. But behind them came the Pharaoh's soldiers and before them lay a great body of water, the Red Sea. There seemed to be no escape.

"The cloud, the cloud. It's moving!" shouted one of the watchmen.

"Look at it," exclaimed another. "It's moving from in front of us to behind us."

"Perfect," cried another. "It will be so dark between us and the Egyptians that they won't be able to see us."

"It's so dark I'm frightened," screamed one woman who couldn't find her family. Sheep bleated, goats cried noisily, babies howled, and children wailed.

"Aaron, Aaron. Speak to God for us and plead our cause," begged the terrified people.

"Moses, Moses, take us to safety," cried the people in panic.

"Miriam, Miriam, plead with the waters to protect us from our enemies," shouted the people in great fright.

"Trust the waters," pleaded Miriam. "Remember what happened before," she said. "The waters protected Moses as a baby when they carried him to safety and to life. If God could do that then the waters of the Red Sea are not here to trap us. Trust the waters to carry us again to safety."

It was so dark that no one saw Moses their leader stretch out his hand over the sea. A mighty wind from the east came up and blew all night. It turned the sea-bed into a marsh. To see how firm it was, Miriam stepped on to the squishy ground. As soon as she took her first step, the waters divided and made a dry path. Everybody struggled to get across the firm land to the safety of the far shore as fast as they could. Fathers and mothers carried tents and food. Children helped the flocks of sheep and herds of goats. They all managed to get across before dawn. Then they sat down in the darkness and rested quietly.

Just before dawn, Moses again stretched out his hand over the sea. The wind went down. The waters returned to where they had always been. There was no firm path any more. Everything was quiet.

Then, suddenly, someone cried out.

"I hear rumbling! Is it thunder?"

"It sounds like people screaming and shouting," warned another. "It's coming from the side of the sea we just left."

It was hard to see. The pillar of cloud covered the sea. Everyone was shouting, trying to make sense of what they were hearing.

"What's that crashing noise?"

"I hear horses neighing and men cursing. I think it's the Egyptians."

"They're trapped by the water."

The Egyptians' chariots were stuck in the marsh and the mud.

They couldn't move. The drivers tried to turn the horses back to the shore, but the horses couldn't budge the heavy chariots. Finally, there was only silence. The pillar of cloud covered the sea. It was still dark.

In the silence, Miriam knew the enemy was drowned. Not one Egyptian was left alive. Her heart grew cold at the thought. She sat quietly by herself for a while.

Then Aaron came by. "Miriam, Miriam. We've won! We've been saved. We've won!"

He dragged her to her feet. She took a tambourine in her hand and invited all the women to celebrate by joining in a circle dance. Miriam led the singing,

"Sing of God who has covered himself in glory,

Horse and rider he has thrown into the sea."

Cymbals clattered and clashed, tambourines jingled and jangled, and children clapped their hands.

The women swirled in circles. In their bright red, yellow, and purple clothing they swung out behind all the men and shouted their joy. The men echoed them with shouts of victory. All the children clapped their hands and whistled and sang and danced.

As each dancer took a step with the left foot, the women shook their tambourines high in the air. Then all took up the song:

"Sing of God who has covered himself in glory.

Horse and rider he has thrown into the sea."

They joined hands and made a huge circle with Miriam and Moses and Aaron and danced most of the night.

As dawn broke, the children started to play games that lasted all day. Some pretended to be the Egyptians. Some played Miriam and Moses. Others were the sheep and the goats. Still others pretended to be the waters of the Red Sea. They played far into the next night. They were allowed to stay up later than ever before.

Miriam
Numbers 12

This Miriam story is included because Miriam played a role sometimes equal in prophecy and leadership to that of Moses. Micah 6:4 mentions Miriam, Moses and Aaron in the same breath. It is not often recognized that she was one of four women (along with Deborah, Huldah, and Noadiah) named as prophetesses in the Hebrew Bible.

This is the story of how Aaron and Miriam rail against Moses' Cushite (Egyptian) wife, who was probably a woman of color, and certainly a non-Hebrew. They also express jealousy over Moses' seemingly exclusive leadership role.

Some commentaries suggest that as punishment for her leading the revolt against Moses' Cushite wife, Miriam is dealt the most severe penalty. She alone is struck with leprosy, a disfiguring skin disease. She is isolated from the people for a week. Israel's law recognized leprosy and skin diseases as a state of impurity. Israelite religion excluded from cultic participation all persons in a state of impurity or uncleanness. They were deemed unholy and had to endure a cleansing within a certain time.

What remains a mystery is why *only* Miriam was struck with leprosy.

Miriam

story by Jim Taylor

His brother Moses was the key
But Aaron spoke for all the three,
Miriam often stood alone,
Because she had a mind of her own.

Moses made a lot of rules. Moses didn't keep all the rules himself.

"You must not marry strangers," he said. But Moses himself had a wife who was a stranger from the land of Cush and a woman of color.

Aaron and Miriam became angry. "Is Moses the only one God speaks through? Didn't God speak through us too?"

Soon everyone was angry. The people started to murmur. The murmur grew. You could hear it around the campfires. You could hear it when Moses gathered the people together to teach them new rules. It grew from a murmur to a mutter, from a mutter to a rumble, from a rumble to a roar.

Everyone could hear it but Moses.

Even God heard it.

God called to Moses, Aaron, and Miriam. "Come out to the Tent of Meeting, all three of you." Only Moses went into this holy place. Miriam and Aaron were terrified. God came to them in a pillar of cloud. Miriam and Aaron fell on their faces to avoid looking at God. And God said, "I chose who I will reveal myself to. Moses is my prophet. I speak face to face with him. How dare you criticize the one whom I have chosen?"

Then the pillar of cloud left them.

Miriam was so angry with God and with Moses that her skin went bright red. And then she went white.

"If you keep making that face," said Moses, "your face might freeze that way."

And it did! When Aaron looked at his sister Miriam, he saw that her skin had turned pure white. As white as snow on the mountain tops. As white as the manna that fell for our food. As white as our clothes, bleached by the desert sun.

Miriam was too proud to ask for favors from her little brother, Moses. But Aaron wasn't – not after he saw what happened to Miriam!

"Please, Moses, don't turn your own sister into a monster, rejected by the people," he pleaded.

So Moses went into the Tent of Meeting by himself and talked to God again. When Moses came out, he said that Miriam would have to leave the camp for a week. She had a disease that made her unclean. No one could talk with her, or hug her, or give her food. She had to be left completely alone.

Then Moses called all the people of the camp together, and told them to leave Miriam alone.

The people began to murmur that this wasn't fair. Everyone had been protesting, but only Miriam got punished.

You could hear the murmuring around the campfires, and when the people came together to listen to Moses.

And the murmur became a mutter, and the mutter became a rumble, and the rumble became a roar.

You could hear it all through the camp. Some of the people sneaked out of the camp in the darkness, to give Miriam food, and water.

And all of the people refused to move on until Miriam was well again, and could come back into the camp.

The Woman Who Talked Back to Jesus
Mark 7:24–30; Matthew 15:21–28

This is a story about a woman who refused to "know her place." She was poor, a foreigner, and a Gentile. In the eyes of many, she had no legitimate claim on God's grace. Yet she demonstrated self-confidence, dignity, and self-assurance in her encounter with Jesus. She is insistent, demanding, and unafraid.

In both gospels in which this story appears, the preceding narratives are about defilement and ritual uncleanness. The nub of the controversy was whether an inclusive table sharing of both Jewish Christians and Gentile Christians was justified in the new Jesus movement. Peter's experience with this same issue is reflected in Galatians 2:11–14 and in his meeting with Cornelius (Acts 10:1–11) How "open" should the Christian community be? How open should it be to women like this Canaanite, who wanted access to God's grace equally with the Jews?

This remains an issue for the contemporary church. What restrictions, laws, customs do we "lay on" those who come seeking God's grace? Is "a mighty fortress is our church" ever justified? The major theologian and spokesperson for inclusive table sharing was a woman, and a foreigner at that!

She was triply oppressed. As a Gentile she was a "dog" to the Jewish purists. Dogs and swine were considered unclean animals, and therefore they could be used to characterize pagans (racist or religious oppression)... as the mother of an afflicted and alienated girl who was helpless (class oppression), and as a woman with whom no decent man, much less a young rabbi, should be talking (sexist oppression). (Samuel Rayan s.j., In Christ: The Power of Women. *India, 1986.)*

The focus of the story is on her courage in speaking to Jesus. She was the protagonist. She came on behalf of her daughter (her future?) who was in bondage to evil, and she expected liberation from Jesus. She took up Jesus' image of the "children-table-housedogs" and challenged it. She countered the argument that the children of Israel should be fed and that their food should not be taken from them and fed to the dogs (Gentiles) by her reference to the abundance of food and grace at Christian table community. She believed the gracious goodness of God is abundant enough for both Jews and Gentiles. Her bold faith moves Jesus to heal (Matthew 15:29–31) and to feed people (Matthew 15:32–39) as God's promises are fulfilled.

She defiantly resisted despair, and exhibited a bold faith in God's promise of steadfast love to all. She may even have used a bit of humor and raised Jesus' consciousness in the process.

For Further Reading

Fiorenza, Elisabeth Schussler. *In Memory of Her*. New York: Crossroad, 1983, p. 137.

Rayan, Samuel, s.j. *In Christ: The Power of Women*. All India Council of Christian Women, Stree Reflect Series 4, Madras, 1986.

Wahlberg, Rachel Conrad. "Jesus and the Uppity Woman." In *Jesus According to a Woman*, New York: Paulist Press, 1975.

The Woman Who Talked Back to Jesus

I'm a person,
Not a mouse,
Not a louse,
Not a souse,
Not a house,
Not a grouse,
But a real live flesh and blood person!

"I knew something was wrong," the mother said to her little girl. The little girl wiggled in her mother's lap.

"You were having terrible temper tantrums. You picked fights with all your friends. You teased the life out of your little brother. You complained of headaches. I didn't know what was wrong. It was as if a demon had got hold of you.

"I heard that Jesus had come to town. He was a Jew, and most Jews didn't have dealings with us Canaanites. I had heard that Jesus was different. He had set a man free from demons and I knew he could do the same for you. I went to the place where I knew Jesus had gone to rest. There was a crowd, so I shouted at the top of my lungs,

'Son of David, take pity on me. Take pity on me. My daughter is tormented by a demon.'

"He didn't answer me! Had he not heard me? He pretended I wasn't even there. So I just kept on shouting.

'Son of David, take pity on me. Take pity on me. My daughter is tormented by a demon.'

"I yelled louder and louder. I knew he could help you."

"Did Jesus tell you to stop shouting at him?" the little girl asked. "You always tell me to stop shouting."

"You're right, I do. Sometimes you're pretty loud," said the little girl's mother. "But no, Jesus didn't tell me to stop shouting. But his disciples were getting nervous. They saw neighbors looking out of their windows, watching us. They said to Jesus, 'Send her away, she is pestering us.'

"But Jesus didn't. Instead, he said to the crowd, 'I was sent only to the lost sheep of Israel.'

"I couldn't believe my ears. Was this the man I'd heard so much about? He might as well have said to me, 'You are an outsider. I only set Jews free.'

"I ran up to him, knelt before him, and begged, 'Help me,

help me. Take pity on me.'

"By this time he had noticed me. He said a strange thing. 'It's not fair to take the children's food and throw it to the dogs.'

"Now I was really angry. Who did he think he was, calling me a dog? I knew I wasn't an important person. I was poor. I was a foreigner. I was a woman. But I also knew I was a person. I was a mother. I was not a dog."

"I would have kicked him in the shin and run away," said the little girl.

"Believe me, I wanted to," said the girl's mother. "But then I thought that maybe he was testing me or maybe he was joking. Either way, I wasn't giving up.

"I went back to him a third time. I stood up straight. I looked him in the eye. I wanted to wink as I said, 'Yes, but even the dogs (meaning me), even the dogs get to eat the scraps which fall from their master's table.'

"I didn't know whether or not he'd find that too sassy, particularly with the sideways look I gave him. Or would he find it kind of funny?"

"Did he?" the little girl asked.

"He did. It seemed to turn him upside down. He loved my courage.

"'Woman,' he said to me, 'you have risked greatly. You have lots of courage. For this saying you may go your way; the demon has left your daughter.'

"I could hardly believe it. I went home and found you lying on the bed. It was true! The demon had left you."

The little girl gave a whoop, jumped off her mother's lap, tore across the room, and outside to play.

The little girl's mother leaned back in her chair, let out a big sigh, and said, "Well, most of the demon, anyway."

The Mystery of the Lost Coin
Luke 15:8–10

This woman who sweeps for a lost coin is a metaphor for God and the repentant sinner. Jesus tells this parable with the woman in God's position, playing out God's role of seeking the lost and rejoicing when the lost is found. This is the main point of the parable.

This short passage is traditionally ignored in favor of the more popular ones of the Lost Sheep and the Prodigal Son, between which it is placed. Yet many children today have never seen a real live sheep. They are, though, quite used to seeing a woman sweeping. How many "woman sweeping" images have you seen in stained glass windows? All these parables make the same point, but this one, featuring a woman and a very familiar image, begs to be told in any book of Bible stories from a woman's perspective.

No one has ever seen God. We therefore speak of the holy in metaphors: "God is like..." The metaphor of God as a woman sweeping is only one of numerous biblical female metaphors. Others are God as nursing mother (Isaiah 49:15, 1 Peter 2:2–3); as midwife (Isaiah 66:4, Psalm 22:9–10); and as a woman giving birth (Isaiah 42:14, Deuteronomy 32:18, Job 38:8, Isaiah 66:13). There are metaphors of God as a female animal: God as mother hen (Isaiah 31:5, Matthew 23:37); as mother eagle (Deuteronomy 32:11–12); and as a she-bear (Hosea 13:8). The Spirit (Romans 8:26) and Dame Wisdom (Proverbs 8ff.) are understood to be female.

Luke places this story in his gospel to reply to the harsh accusation that Jesus "receives sinners and eats with them," (Luke 15:2). The emphasis of the story is on the joy of finding the lost coin, *not* on the search. It was told to jolt the hearer into realizing that God acts like this woman, tirelessly seeking her lost coin, and joyously, finding it. Thus it is with God's own concern, which Jesus demonstrated by joyously sharing the table with sinners, outcasts, and other "undesirables."

The Mystery of the Lost Coin

Little precious lost coin,
Wherever can you be?
I will sweep, and sweep again,
Until my coin I see.

How would you feel if you found something special that you had lost? Here's a story Jesus told one day. He was in a little village visiting with all kinds of people – the poor, the lame, tax collectors and sinners. This is the story he told.

Once there was a woman who lived in a small village. She lived in a little square whitewashed house. Its tiny windows, high up in the walls, made the house rather dark. But the small windows kept out the sunshine when it was very, very hot, and kept out the cold winds in the winter. On the outside of the house, a little stairway ran up to the flat roof. People used the roof of the house just like a room. It was a lovely place to go in the evening when the air was cool.

Inside the small house the cooking pots and water jugs stood in one corner. In the big box beside the wall, the woman kept her best clothes and treasures.

But there was one treasure the woman did not keep in her big box – ten shiny silver coins. Her coins were her money. They had been given to her when she got married. They were all the money she had, and were very valuable. She would need them if the rains failed to water the seeds in her garden and she wouldn't have enough corn to eat.

She wore the coins in a row on her forehead band. Each coin had been sewn individually to the band.

One day, as she went about her work, she put her hand up to her forehead and found that one of her coins was gone! What had happened?

"I'm sure it was there this morning," she thought. "Perhaps it dropped off as I was walking to the well."

So she hurried out of the house and went back along the path to the well, looking at the ground all the way, hoping to find her lost coin.

"What is the matter?" her friends asked her as they saw her looking on the ground.

"Oh," she said, "I have lost one of my silver coins."

So her friends came to help her look. They searched and searched but they couldn't find the lost coin.

Holding back her tears, the woman went home. She thought of all the places where her coin might have dropped.

"Maybe it fell into the corn," she thought. So she picked up her basket where she kept the corn, and brought it out into the daylight. She sifted and sifted the corn and bumped the little basket on the ground to make sure that it was quite empty. But the lost coin was not there.

"Perhaps I rolled it in my sleeping mat," she thought. She lifted her mat, took it outside the house and shook it. But the coin wasn't there. She emptied all the water pots and turned her cooking pots upside down. But the lost coin was not there either. Finally she went down on her knees and felt all about the floor of her little house. She ran her fingers into every corner. But there was no coin.

"I'm going to light a lamp and look again," she thought. So she lit a lamp and looked in all parts of her house. Still there was no coin.

Her friends came around to ask if she had found it. They were sorry when she said, "No. I haven't found it yet."

"Keep looking," said one of her friends. "It must be somewhere in your house or nearby."

So with her lamp burning brightly, the woman took her broom and began sweeping, sweeping, sweeping her house. She swept every nook and cranny. Her little house had never been so clean.

She lifted all her pots and bowls and swept behind them into the very darkest corner – but still she could not find her coin. She put her pots back again and swept around the doorstep.

"Whatever am I going to do?" she thought. "I've looked everywhere."

But then she remembered that she had not looked behind her big wooden treasure box. The box was so heavy she couldn't lift it. But she tried very hard, and managed to push it out a little from the wall. There was a lot of dust behind it. She put the lamp on the box to give her light, and began sweeping again. Suddenly she thought she saw something glitter. She lifted the lamp and bent down to look behind the box. And then – she saw it plainly. It was her shining silver coin.

"Look," she cried as she ran to the door. The coin shone brightly in the brilliant sunlight.

"Look," she called out to her friends.

"Look," she whooped to anyone who was in the street.

"Look," she shouted to the hills.

"Look," they echoed back.

"Look. I have found the coin I had lost. I have found it. Let's have a party."

So all her friends came, and many others who heard the music, or who had heard her shouting. All were welcome. The little house was full of joy that night, because the coin that had been lost had been found.

Helen's Coin

based on the "real life" experience of Helen Mathers, Kingston

Helen had a very special coin collection. The coins were English coins, and there were 15 in all. Some of the coins were silver. The two smallest coins were copper. The biggest coin was called the crown. The very smallest coin was called the farthing. It was smaller than a nickel. Helen's coins were called "specimen" coins, because each one was rare. She kept them in a velvet lined box that had a satin space for each coin. They were different from ordinary coins. They had been issued at the Coronation of the British King George VI in 1937. They were precious and would have been worth a lot of money if she had ever sold them. Hardly anyone else had such coins.

Helen's son Alistair took them to school one day. He wanted to show them to his classmates. He was in grade two and was seven years old. He promised his mother not to open the box that held the coins until he was safely inside his classroom.

When Alistair returned home after school, he could hardly hold back his tears. One of the coins was missing. Where it should have been in the velvet box there was only an empty satin space. He didn't know how or where it had been lost. He wondered how he could tell his mother it was lost.

When he did, she was sad. With one of the coins missing, the entire collection wasn't special any more.

It was Friday. Helen and Alistair hurried off to the school. They found the janitor who had just finished sweeping the class-room with his big white broom. They searched every nook and cranny of the school room. The caretaker showed them where he had dropped all his sweepings. It was a huge garbage can, filled with gum, paper, broken pencils, and someone's tooth.

Helen sifted through the garbage. There was no coin to be found. She remembered the Bible story of the woman sweeping and cleaning her house until she found her lost coin. How wonderful it would be if she could find her lost coin!

She hunted through the schoolroom again. Alistair helped her move the chairs and the desks, but they found nothing. She picked up each book from the shelf to see if the coin had fallen down between the books. She looked under the teacher's desk, and felt around the floor with her hand. But the coin was not to be found.

They went home, feeling sad and unhappy.

On Monday morning, Alistair ran home from school. Under his arm he had a big piece of cardboard, wrapped round and round with a whole roll of Scotch tape.

"Mother, Mother it's here. The coin is here," he shouted.

Helen tore the tape off. There was the lost coin, glittering and shining as though it had never been lost.

"A boy found it in the schoolyard," said Alistair. "He knew it was yours, so he brought it to me this morning. The teacher fixed it on the cardboard so I wouldn't lose it again."

"Wonderful," Helen gasped. "It's wonderful to have this coin back again. Without it, the coin collection wouldn't be the same."

"I'm so happy," shouted Alistair, "I feel so good inside." He did cartwheels around the living room.

Their house was full of joy that night, because the coin that had been lost had been found.

House Church
(Acts and the Epistles)

The women leaders in the Greek scriptures did not just fall out of the sky. There were openings and a relative degree of freedom for women at the time of Jesus. The American theologian Bernadette Brooten, having researched the position of women in the early synagogues, found that

> There existed a number of women leaders. They emerged and came to the Jesus movement because they were already questioning their own culture. Jesus awakened, supported and strengthened their desire to be set free. (Reinheld Traitler, in "Biblical Perspectives on Patriarchy" in Speaking for Ourselves. Geneva: WCC, 1990, p. 62.)

In the early Christian movement, women exercised leadership as missionaries, founders of Christian communities, apostles, prophets, and leaders of house churches, according to the scholarship of Elisabeth Schussler Fiorenza (Fiorenza, "Women in Pre-patriarchal and Patriarchal Churches," in Union Theological Seminary Review. Vol. 33 No. 3, 4, 1978, p. 155–158).

When Paul appeared on the scene, there were already a number of women-led communities, and Paul met women of acknowledged status who were actively engaged in mission independently of him. To do Paul justice, he confirmed, valued, and stressed their leadership importance. In Romans 16, a passage that names 26 colleagues of Paul, at least ten are women. In Philippian (4:2) and Colossians (4:15) Paul names three more women. These active collaborators were Phoebe, Prisca, Mary, Junia, Tryphaena, Tryphosa, Persis, the mother of Rufus, Julia, the sister of Nereus, Eudia, Syntche, and Nympha. Prisca and Aquila, Junia and her partner Andronicus, had become Christians before Paul had (Romans 16:7). They apparently worked with him in Antioch and even shared imprisonment with him.

Neither Junia nor Prisca are identified as "wives," even though they worked in team ministry with their spouses. Remarkably, they are noted as leaders in their own right. Paul stresses that they were outstanding members of the circle of apostles.

Phoebe is given the titles diakonos (deacon) and prostatis (president or governor). Tradition has taken great pains to play down the significance of both titles because they were given to a woman. Nevertheless, Phoebe founded house churches, traveled widely, and played a leading role in the early communities.

Christians in the early days met in houses for worship. Traveling missionaries and house churches were central to the early Christian movement which depended upon mobility and patronage. Women functioned in both missionary and house church operations. House churches provided opportunities for women to play a leading role in ministry.

Elisabeth Schussler Fiorenza, for example, thinks that the much maligned Martha of the gospels (Luke 10:38–42) was a strong leader of a house church.

As the owner, Martha welcomes the Lord into her house. The text does not say that Martha is in the kitchen preparing and serving a meal but that she is preoccupied with diakonia and diakonein, terms that in Luke's time had already become technical terms for ecclesial leadership... In early Christian usage, diakonia refers to eucharistic table service in the housechurch... but also included the proclamation of the word. (Elisabeth Schussler Fiorenza, "A Feminist Critical Interpretation for Liberation: Martha and Mary: Luke 10:38–42," in Religion and Intellectual Life, *Vol. III, No. 2, Winter, 1986, pp. 21–31.)*

The shift in the second century from house church to church as the "household of God," with its attendant transfer of authority to local officers of the church, signaled the emergence of what were to become bishops and clergy. Only male heads of households were eligible for these administrative and financial functions. Consequently, women were increasingly deprived of their role in ministry.

Here follow a few stories on these themes. You may want to write a story of one of these early church leaders (Phoebe or Junia) for your children. There are extensive writings on the subject. Here are a few suggestions.

For Further Reading

Fiorenza, Elisabeth Schussler. *In Memory of Her – A Feminist Theological Reconstruction of Christian Origins.* New York: Crossroad, 1983.

Heine, Susanne. *Women and Early Christianity: Are the Feminist Scholars Right?* London: SCM, 1987.

Women and Early Christianity: A Reappraisal. Minneapolis: Augsburg, 1988.

Laporte, Jean. *The Role of Women in Early Christianity.* New York: Mellen, 1982.

With or Without a Cross

This story is about the experience of Christian people in China who, after the 1950 communist revolution and the closure of church buildings, met for years in homes and other private places for prayer and worship. In the mid 1980s churches were returned to the people, but the tradition of meeting as house churches still remains.

In 1980, Chinese Christian leaders looked back 30 years and affirmed the important role played by women in the house church movement. The house churches were fellowships of joy and suffering. They were not free from quarrels or jealousy. But they were – and continue to be – part of God's faithful community in China.

House churches are important in the 1990s, as the "Church of Christ In Formation" in China takes historical shape, and as the China Christian Council re-joins the World Council of Churches international Christian community.

I have adapted this story from a small book, *Households of God on China's Soil* by Raymond Fung (WCC Mission series, Geneva 1982). The book gives reliable information on 19 house churches scattered in seven provinces of China.

With or Without a Cross

My name is Siu May. I am ten years old. I live in China. Everyone knows my mother was a Jesus believer. After the church buildings were closed in my village, Christians met in our house.

We began with 14 people, all women. My mother owned a silver family cross. We always began our meetings with that cross in the middle of our living room. We put it on a stool. My mother was the leader. We prayed. We read the Bible. We sang hymns. The hours passed quietly.

Then we had hard times in China. Our attendance dropped to four people. Several people couldn't come to worship because they had to work.

My mother suggested that families could come together for supper. Everyone could bring his or her rice or fish. It would save fuel. Our numbers jumped to 20. I guess everyone liked to eat together. It was a good time to play with the other kids while our parents visited.

News spread about our common meal. One day five families joined our group. Of course they didn't come to pray. They brought a little rice with them, but they ate more than they brought. I watched them. These families never came back a second time although we never stopped them. They were ashamed to return.

Then someone stole the silver cross. For several months there was no cross. So I made a new one. I put two short twigs together and wrapped them with a woollen cloth and sewed it up. The cross fit the palm of my hand.

One day I put my cross in the middle of our family table. My mother led the family in the Lord's Prayer.

My brother, who was 20 years old, had not lived at home for four years. He had not been part of our house church. He had not been part of a Christian group for those four years. He had now lost his job and his own house. When he came back, he could only remember a few phrases of the Lord's Prayer. I helped him remember. I gave him my homemade cross.

The Cheng family have joined our house church. Now we are 40. It's too crowded. Soon we'll get our church building back again. We meet every week in my house, with or without a cross. We will probably keep on meeting in our house, even when our church building is returned to us. I like our house church.

Thecla

A first century oral tradition, formalized in *The Acts of Paul and Thecla* (Vol. 8 in *The Anti-Nicene Fathers,* Alexander Roberts and James Donaldson ed., New York: Scribners, 1885-1897) devotes itself to the story of a woman missionary, Thecla. During the first three centuries of the church's life, many regions regarded this book as part of the canon of scripture. At the beginning of the third century, women in Carthage still appealed to the apostle Thecla for women's authority to preach and baptize. The book mentions many women. Our story is about one of them, and is an adaptation of the legend/story also recorded by Elisabeth Schussler Fiorenza. Legends flourish and grow up around significant persons and should not be dismissed lightly.

This story was told to emphasize women as men's spiritual equals, and depicted women as free from sex stereotyping. Because Thecla chose not to marry and adopted a most unconventional role for a woman, she was persecuted.

The story said Thecla could preach, but none of her sermons was recorded. Several of her prayers were quoted. Women could apparently be tolerated as prayer leaders but not as itinerant missionaries preaching the gospel.

This story is included because it emphasizes the significant leadership role of women in the early church. Thecla appears not as an isolated heroine, but as one of many women. Two fierce lionesses, who contributed to her deliverance, remind us once more of our interdependence with the non-human world.

For Further Reading

Fiorenza, Elisabeth Schussler. *In Memory of Her.* New York: Crossroad, 1983.

Ruether, Rosemary Radford. *Woman-guides – Toward a Feminist Theology.* Boston: Beacon Press, 1985.

Thecla

Many years ago there was a woman called Thecla. She became a Christian after hearing the preaching of a very famous man, Paul.

When she announced she would never marry, her family was upset. The man who had intended to marry her didn't like it either. He complained to the governor about Thecla's refusal to marry him. The governor put Thecla into prison. Then he ordered her to be burned at the stake. First he drove Paul out of the city. Then he had a fire set to burn Thecla.

Thecla stood in the middle of the great blazing fire, made the sign of the cross, but was not burned! A great cloud of water and hail came and put the fire out.

One day a huge earthquake threw the village into confusion. Thecla escaped and joined Paul in a distant city. She began to preach. In that same city lived Queen Tryphena, a close friend of the Emperor Caesar. Thecla had spoken the word of God so strongly that Queen Tryphena and all of her servants had become Christian. The queen's own daughter had died, so she wanted to look after Thecla.

Later, a man called Alexander, listened to Thecla's preaching, and fell in love with her. But Thecla told him she had decided never to marry. He was very angry. He got strong men to throw her into the arena where she would have to fight for her life against the wild beasts – bears, lions, and fierce lionesses.

They tied Thecla to a fierce lioness. But the lioness, with Thecla sitting upon her back, licked Thecla's feet.

"Let her free," some of the people cried. But others shouted, "Away with her. Let her be killed."

The people then stripped off Thecla's clothing and threw her back into the arena. A second lioness, which was supposed to have eaten Thecla, stopped dead in her tracks. Instead of attacking Thecla, the lioness came and lay down at Thecla's feet. The women cried with joy. A fierce lion, trained to eat men, charged Thecla. Another lioness chased him out of the arena. The bear ran up to attack Thecla but the lioness tore the bear to pieces.

Thecla was frightened. She was sure she was going to die. She prayed. She saw a ditch full of water in the arena. She baptized herself with the water. A cloud of fire came to Thecla so people couldn't see her naked. Nor could any wild beasts harm her.

Queen Tryphena fainted. Some of the people thought she was dead, so the governor stopped the games at once.

Alexander, who had wanted Thecla to marry him, begged the governor to set Thecla free. Alexander was afraid that the Emperor Caesar would be angry that his friend Queen Tryphena had died and would destroy the whole city.

So Thecla got her clothes back and was set free. All the women shouted with a loud voice.

"God has delivered Thecla." The women shouted so loud that the city shook with the sound.

Queen Tryphena had not died. She had only fainted. She went to meet Thecla.

"I give you all that is mine," she said. Thecla took the lionesses, and became part of the family of Tryphena.

After a short while, Thecla followed Paul to a place called Myra. In Myra the people chose her to preach the word of God.

Priscilla and Aquila, who had become Christians long before Paul had, came from Jerusalem for the ceremony. So did Phoebe, an apostle famous for her work in starting house churches.

For the rest of her life Thecla preached and baptized people in many other places.

Rosie and Chris

A Postscript to Thecla

"Rosie," shouted Chris, "Come and play church."

They were playing in Rosie's attic. The attic was full of boxes covered in dust. Old winter coats and sweaters hung from a clothes line strung between two rafters. There was an old chair with a big white sheet draped over it. Chris pulled the sheet off the chair and wrapped it around himself.

"This can be my gown, just like the minister's," he said. Then he stacked up three boxes, one on top of the other, for a pulpit.

"Come on," Chris urged. "Let's get Charlie. He's just a baby. I can baptize him. You can bring me the basin of water. Then you can take him out when it's time for me to preach. Babies cry a lot you know. And then you can get the coffee hour ready after church."

"No," Rosie shouted. She stamped her foot. "I won't play church with you unless I can baptize and preach too. It's not just men who do those things. Mommy does them too."

Soon they were yelling at the tops of their lungs. They were so loud that their mother heard them, and she was all the way downstairs. "I should probably go check on them," she said to herself. She put down her book and climbed the stairs to the attic.

"What's all the noise about?" she asked.

"Chris wants to play church but he won't let me do any of the good stuff like preaching or baptizing," complained Rosie.

Chris' face got real red.

"Just because Mom does it, doesn't mean all women can. It doesn't mean you can. Mom's special," cried Chris.

"Enough you two," she said. "There were women preaching and baptizing long before I ever did. There was Thecla and Phoebe and Priscilla for starters."

Rosie crossed her arms and gave Chris her best "so there" look. Chris was quiet for a minute. He hated to lose an argument but he wanted to play the game even more.

"Well," he said finally, "okay."

Then he got an idea.

"We could take turns!" He went to the clothes hanging from the line, took down a bright red spring coat.

"Hey Rosie, how about a red robe for you?" he said and tossed the coat to Rosie.

Women Set Free

If there is one image that women the world over share, it is the image of the "bent-over" woman. The following stories reflect the experience of women as bent over, that is, as weighed down or hemmed in by systems beyond their control. These stories also show women beginning to stand tall as they are set free from burdens. They are stories of hope.

The Woman Who Was Set Free
Luke 13:10–17

The traditional interpretation of Luke 13:12, "Woman, you are loosed from your ailment," has been that the woman was healed of a disease by Jesus.

However, Rev. Lee Oo-Chung, a South Korean theologian, points out that when Jesus says, "Woman, you have been set free from your ailment," the Greek word *apoluo*, which means "to set free" is used, not the word *therapuo* which means to heal a disease. This means that the woman was not sick nor did she have a hunched back. It means she is bent over by all kinds of societal pressures.

This story describes the transformation and liberation of a woman who was "bound by Satan." Satan represents all evil powers that keep humans in bondage – cultures, laws, traditions, and economic systems or political powers that oppress women. She cannot "look up." She is without hope.

When the woman is finally able to look up, she sees the coming order of things. She is restored to hope. The Greek word used in this story in Luke 13:11 is the same one used in Luke 21:28: "Look up and raise your heads, because your redemption is drawing near." "You have been set free" is announced in the passive voice as something already completed before Jesus' intervention. The woman responds by praising God, not by thanking Jesus.

The story is positioned between the healing of the man with the withered hand, and the man with dropsy. Crippled bodies and crippled souls are bound together. Three stories in a row say the same thing. They point to a company of men and women who stand upright in the presence of Jesus, enjoying equal status and hope.

Theologian Elisabeth Schussler Fiorenza thinks the original story was not told to make a point against the Pharisees. That appears to be a later Christian interpretation, and carries tones of anti-Semitism. Jewish interpreters of the law agreed that saving the life of either animals or humans was allowed on the Sabbath. The full intention of the Sabbath of the Torah was "to praise the goodness of Israel's creator God." Jesus' action liberates the woman to do just that. Our story has the woman's transformation as the focus, not the added theological debate. Our story then, deals only with Luke 13:11–13.

This biblical story should be told together with "The Woman Who Carried a Load," and "Susan Laughed."

For Further Reading

Fiorenza, Elisabeth Schussler. "Interpretation for Liberation and Transformation." Bellarmine Lecture, 1989, Harvard Divinity School, U.S.A.

Wahlberg, Rachel Conrad. *Jesus and the Freed Woman*, New York: Paulist Press, 1978, p. 15.

The Woman Who Was Set Free

from an idea of Rev. Lee Oo-Chung, South Korea

Here is the woman (Bend over)
Here is the sun (Circle with hands)
Here is Jesus (Show hands)
New life has begun! (Raise hands in praise)

A woman was bent over. She could not straighten her back. She could not stand up straight. Her face was constantly turned towards the ground. She could see only what was at her feet. No matter how bright the sun was, she couldn't look at it. No matter how fleecy the clouds were, she couldn't see them. All she could see was her own dark shadow, cast by the sunshine on her back.

She kept out of the center of things. She often felt cold and lonely. She was afraid people might notice her. Children made fun of her. When she heard the birds twitter, she wondered if they were talking about her. Most people never noticed her, because she stayed on the edge of crowds.

She was not sick. But for some reason she could not straighten herself. She felt as if all the dragons of the sea and the beasts of the forest were riding on her back. She had been like that for 18 long years.

But Jesus noticed her. He called her over. He took both her hands in his. He looked her in the eye.

"Woman, you have been set free from being bent over." Right away she was able to stand up straight.

"I can see the sun," she yelled.

"I can watch the clouds in the sky," she whooped.

"I can follow the birds in their flight," she roared.

It had been a long long time since she had seen another person face to face as she now saw Jesus. And when she heard the birds twitter she no longer feared they were talking about her.

"I can stand up straight," she shouted with excitement. And she thanked God.

Note for Adults. You may want to finish the story. What did the woman do next ?

The Woman Who Carried a Load

This story is drawn from the experience of Latin American churches where most women are marginalized, not only because they are women, but because they are the poorest of the poor. They are "bent over" by international economic structures beyond their control. Much of the wealth that could be theirs is used to pay the interest on their country's debt to foreign governments. This story challenges the oppressive structures of a given society through the weakest, most vulnerable member of that society – a woman. The liberation of the woman is a sign of the coming realm of God. By implication, it unmasks the dehumanizing economic and political systems that keep women in poverty.

The story is set in a slum of Montevideo, Uruguay, visited by Canadian theological students in 1986. It was Maria Teresa Porcile Santiso, a Roman Catholic lay theologian, who first introduced me to Elsa, from whose life this story is adapted.

The Woman Who Carried a Load

Elsa was born poor. She lived in the city in a small house with two rooms and a tar-paper roof. She had 11 children and only two chairs. There was never enough food.

When her husband died, Elsa had even less money than before. She had to pack up her few belongings and move with her children outside the city to a place where all the very poor people lived. She built a hut with plastic and tin. It stood in a sea of mud. She found an old car seat with springs in it and used it as a bed. In front of her hut was a dirty smelly pool of water. Her children were usually sick. They had runny noses. They cried a lot. They were always hungry. They never laughed. There was no school. She felt as though she carried a heavy load on her back.

Every night she went to the city garbage dump and sorted through the garbage. She brought back anything she could use to keep her children alive. Sometimes she got work carrying gravel on her back to build roads. This went on for 18 years.

Elsa was so ashamed that she always looked down at the ground to avoid other people's eyes.

"There goes the bent-over woman," the children of the city screamed and taunted, as they saw her go by carrying her load.

One day, a young woman came to the place where Elsa lived. She wore a cross around her neck. She talked with Elsa and the other women about how poor they were. They wondered why they weren't rich like people in the nearby city. The young woman asked if she could read them a story from the Bible.

At first, they said no.

"The last story we heard from the Bible said we would always be poor and the reader told us that it was God's will," said Elsa.

"This is quite a different story," said the young woman. "Listen." Then the young woman told them the story of the bent-over woman in Luke's gospel.

"That's my story," exclaimed Elsa. "I'm bent over because I'm so poor. It's not my fault. It's the way things are here."

"We can't stand up straight either," said the other women. "The poverty and disease weigh us down. The city children make fun of us."

"That story you told us means that God doesn't want us to live like this," said another woman.

"Let's change what we can," someone suggested.

So they joined hands and went to work for and with each other.

Elsa was in charge of a large cooking pot. Each day the women filled the pot with the few vegetables and water that they had managed to gather together. One brought peas. One brought corn. Many brought potatoes. Elsa shared some beans. Another brought turnips.

"Couldn't we leave the turnips out?" whined one child.

Into the pot they tossed the lot: the peas, the corn, the potatoes, the beans. But they left the turnips out!

The pot stood on a high fireplace, and Elsa had to straighten up her back and stretch to reach the top so she could stir the stew. Her back gradually began to unbend.

"Sniff-sniff." A wonderful smell filled the air. It tickled the noses of the children. Their mouths began to water as they chanted together, "Into the pot we tossed the lot: the peas, the corn, the potatoes, the beans. But we left the turnips out."

They lined up, and held out their rusty tin-can plates for a bite to eat.

It seemed to them that the birds began to sing more sweetly. The leaves of the trees danced and rustled in fresh breezes. And Elsa stood up straighter and looked people in the eye.

One day there was a party for everyone. Elsa's 11 children hung balloons from the ceiling of the small community shelter. The woman with a cross around her neck worked with them. The women served pan-fried cakes, brownies, empanadas (meat pies) and tea. All the children laughed and stuffed themselves with food. Especially Elsa's 11! All the little girls and boys stood up straight and played the circle game "Ring around a Rosie."

"This is how God wants people to live," Elsa thought to herself, "standing straight, in a circle. And laughing."

Susan Laughed
A Canadian Story

Canadian women are "bent over" too. The statistics are alarming: one in ten women is battered by her husband or male partner; three-quarters of all wife assaults involve a physical attack; six percent involve guns or knives; an average of 100 women a year are murdered by their male partners; 80 percent of the women incarcerated under federal jurisdiction have had a history of physical or sexual abuse; 80 percent of the aboriginal women surveyed on reserves in Ontario have experienced violence.

A study of women with disabilities found almost half had been sexually abused as children, and one in four had been sexually assaulted as an adult. Statistics for violence against children are not yet fully documented (Sources: Status of Women – Canada, Ontario Native Women's Association 1989).

For Further Reading

"Family Violence in a Patriarchal Culture." Published jointly by The Church Council on Justice and Corrections and the Canadian Council on Social Development, Ottawa, Ont. K1Y 4G1, September, 1988.

Susan Laughed

A Canadian Story

Mom was bent double,
Her life at an end,
But God gave life,
And helped her to mend.

There was once a little girl who never laughed. Her name was Susan. When Susan heard or saw her father coming home from work she always ran and crouched in a dark corner upstairs. She couldn't see what was happening downstairs but she could hear.

"Crash. Wham." She heard china plates shatter into a thousand pieces as they were thrown against the kitchen wall.

"Slap. Bang." She heard her mother cry with pain.

Sometimes her mother screamed that she was going to leave this place and live somewhere else. That usually meant still another beating. Susan was afraid.

Susan and her mother always went to church on Sunday. They sat in the back of the church. Her mother held her head in her arms, and her back was bent over. They wouldn't talk to people at the church. Her mother became sadder and sadder. So did Susan. Her mother never smiled. Neither did Susan. One Sunday her mother started to sob, and Susan ran and brought her some Kleenex. She put her hands on her mother's head and tried to lift it. But she wasn't strong enough. Her mother's head remained bent.

One night, her father came home early. He was angry that dinner wasn't ready, even though it wasn't time for dinner. When Susan heard him come home, she hid herself upstairs in the laundry basket. Her mother called her to come down to eat.

Susan's father exploded with fury at her mother.

"Why didn't you cook these vegetables so they're decent to eat," he raged. He slammed his fork and knife down on the table and threw his plate full of food to the floor.

Susan began to cry. Her father grabbed her by the wrist, hit her on the cheek, and roared, "Don't you start. One crybaby in this house is quite enough."

Susan escaped and ran upstairs to her room. She hid under her bed. She heard more slaps and cries, and the slam of the front door. Then silence, except for sobs. When she crept downstairs, she saw her mother lying on the floor holding her head and crying softly to herself.

Later that night, before her father came home again, Susan's mother packed up a few things in a suitcase and took Susan to a new house. It was called a "safe house," and there were lots of other mommies and children there.

At first Susan was sad. She missed her father. She missed her bedroom. She never laughed. But then she made new friends. There were lots of new toys at the "safe house" which the children shared. No one ever beat her mother at the "safe house." Slowly her mother began to lift up her head. She began to look at other people. Her back began to unbend. She began to stand up straighter.

People at the church noticed that Susan and her mother were not so sad as they had been. Susan and her mother began to talk to people. They made friends there. That made Susan feel better.

One wonderful Sunday, when she went into the living room of the "safe house" she heard her mother laugh. Susan was so delighted that she laughed too. And she was no longer afraid.

The Woman Who Did a No-No
Mark 5:25–34

This story is about the woman with the flow of blood, a woman who broke a social taboo.

The traditional interpretation of the story found in Mark 5:25–34 has taught that humility, followed by gratitude, is appropriate behavior for women. But as Lee Oo-Chung, a Korean theologian, points out, women doing theology out of women's struggles understand it as being about breaking taboos of tradition, culture, or religion, and being restored to community.

It is not about healing from a "disease." Both the *New English Bible* and the *J. B. Philips* translation render Mark 5:34, "Be free from your trouble." The *New Jerusalem Bible* says, "Be free from your complaint." This story deals with taking a risk – the risk of being blamed for breaking anything that social or religious custom defines as taboo.

Although the woman knew her flow of blood had stopped when she touched Jesus, the text says she still "trembled and feared" when Jesus asked "who touched me?" If the incident simply involved physical healing, the woman would not have responded with fear and trembling to Jesus' inquiry. But she had broken a taboo. She had been a social reject for 12 years. Religious law declared any "touching," of either the woman or anything associated with her, ritually unclean, that is, taboo (Leviticus 15:19–30). She trembled because she had broken the law (Leviticus 12:2–7). She had sinned by appearing in a public place when she was ritually polluted.

This attitude is not limited to biblical Israel. In India, even today, Hindu women are sent outside their homes at the time of their monthly menstrual period (Christian Conference of Asia Paper, 1986). In Ghana, women used to be considered abnormal during their menstrual period. They had to live alone in the "house for menstruating women" on the outskirts of the village (Potter and Pobee in *New Eyes for Reading*, WCC, Geneva, p. 3).

Imagine the woman working up her courage to touch Jesus' clothes. The Greek word *elegen* is used, indicating that she said over and over and over again, "If I but touch his clothes..." She knew she would be blamed if she decided to break the taboo.

Interestingly, the Greek word for touch, *haptomai*, has the same root as *hapto*, which means lighting a fire. The touching implied a creative joining of two substances so as to create energy.

Jesus could have ignored the touch. He asked "Who touched my clothes?" to make the "touching" public. The disciples tried to put him off. But he looked all around to see who had done it. He persisted in seeking out the woman. Why didn't he just let her remain anonymous? No doubt he knew she had broken a taboo, and would suffer grievous consequences. He must have wanted her deed made public, so other women could benefit by it.

After she had "told him the whole truth," he declared that her faith, her ability to risk, her decision to break a traditional, religious, cultural taboo, had made her whole (or "safe" as one Greek meaning has it). She had reclaimed her humanity and been set free from her trouble.

"Your faith has made you whole" was an early baptismal formula for Christians.

About Taboos

Not to have a child is taboo in Asia. Commonly, the mother of the husband lives with the young couple. Often the woman is blamed for childlessness; too often the husband's mother supports her son unconditionally. This is part of a pattern from which women are yearning to be freed.

In most of the world – not just in Asia – it is believed that a woman, to be completely fulfilled, must bear a child, and particularly a boy.

Every society has its taboos for women. In many, blood has a negative connotation. In this story, blood has a positive meaning. Women have the power to create life; the sign of this ability is their flow of blood. With the restoration of that cycle, this woman could go and live in shalom.

You may want to talk about Canadian taboos for children with the child to whom you read this story. Some of these taboos may be imposed by adults, some by their peers. This discussion will help the child realize that the story is about a woman strong enough to break through a taboo, and not just about a woman being healed from sickness. It may help the child be more transparent about the taboos perceived through his or her own eyes.

The Woman
Who Did a No-No

There was once a woman who was afraid to touch people she loved. Touching people was a no-no. People said it was because she had something bad in her blood. She had been bleeding a little bit for a long long time. She was told she was dirty.

She didn't feel good about herself.

"We can't help you," said the doctors.

"Stay away from us," echoed the people in her village. "You are unclean. It's against the rules to touch us. Stay inside your own house. No one wants to be near you."

The woman was afraid to make friends or to go out among crowds of people.

"The people think I'm disgusting and dirty," she thought to herself. "What can I do? I'm so poor. I've spent all my money on treatments to make me better. But I'm getting worse."

One day, Jesus came to her village.

She had heard about Jesus. "I know I'm not supposed to touch anyone. It's a no-no. But if only I could touch him," she said to herself, "I would be all right. I know it."

She wrung her hands and bit her lip. She was afraid to join the huge crowd that surrounded him. Somebody might recognize her, and push her aside, or tell her to go home.

She didn't know what to do. In despair, she sat down by the side of the road. She pulled her cloak up over her head to hide her face so no one would recognize her. She looked like a bundle of old rags, dumped at the side of the road.

"If only I could touch him," she repeated to herself, over and over. "I've got to do it. Then I'll be all right."

The crowd came moving up the street. They surrounded Jesus. They didn't even notice the bundle of old rags squatting on the road. The people poured around her, like a stream around a rock.

Peeking out, she saw Jesus' feet coming closer. "If only I can touch him, I'll be all right," she repeated again. "I know it."

She screwed up her courage. She reached out and caught the tip of his clothes with two fingers. Then she quickly drew her hand back, before anyone noticed.

Jesus was the first person she had touched for a long time. Right away she felt better. She knew she was better. But she still crouched like a bundle of rags on the road.

Jesus turned around to the crowd and asked, "Who touched my clothes?"

The woman didn't move.

Jesus' disciples answered, "Look at this crowd all around you. Everyone is touching you!"

But Jesus knew someone special had touched his clothes. He looked all around to see who had done it.

The woman knew she was the one he was looking for. Shaking and trembling, she crept forward to him. She knew she had done a no-no. She was afraid to speak. But Jesus kept looking. So she flung herself at his feet, and told him her whole story.

To her great surprise, Jesus didn't send her home. He didn't scold her. He touched her! He took her hands and raised her to her feet. She stood up straight. He looked her in the face. He didn't think she was dirty. Everyone was watching, but she didn't care any more.

Finally Jesus spoke so everyone could hear.

"Daughter," he said, "Your faith has made you safe and whole. Go to your home and village in peace. Be free from your trouble."

And the woman was never again afraid to touch those she loved.

Hugging

There was once a woman whose name was Emily Smith. She was afraid to touch other people, even those she loved. And she *never* hugged anyone. She knew it was a no-no. It was because she had something bad in her blood. The doctors said she had AIDS. Other people said that AIDS made her dirty to other people. She didn't feel good about herself.

"We can't help you," said the doctors.

"Stay away from us," echoed the people on her street. "We know your blood disease could infect us. We don't want you to touch any of us. Just stay inside your house. No one wants to be near you or touch you."

Her friends never came to see her. She was afraid to go among crowds of people.

"Everyone thinks I'm disgusting and dirty," thought the woman to herself. "What shall I do? I've spent all my money to get rid of AIDS but there is no cure. And no one will come near me or touch me, for fear of catching AIDS from me. My friends say that touching me is a no-no."

One day, Emily Smith heard about the Knudson family, who were friendly with people with AIDS. She found out where they lived and went to visit them.

"If only one of them would touch me," she thought. "It would make me feel so human again. No one can catch AIDS by touching me."

She arrived at the Knudsons' house. A little girl called Louise opened the door and asked her to come in. Louise's father welcomed her, and introduced her to the little girl's mother, who was lying on the couch, looking very tired and thin. Louise had gone over to her and given her a big hug. Emily Smith was startled.

"I thought it was a no-no to touch anyone with AIDS," she blurted out. "Aren't you afraid your little girl will catch it from her?" Emily asked Louise's father.

"Yes, she has AIDS," said Louise's father. "But we know that you can't 'catch' AIDS by touching. We know there's nothing to fear from hugging or touching each other."

"In fact," said the woman on the couch, "I feel so much better when my little girl touches me. I feel like a new person. How about another hug darling?" she teased as she grabbed Louise for another hug.

Emily Smith loved the Knudson family. She visited them many many times. They became good friends. And now, whenever Emily arrived at the door, Louise gave her a big hug. Emily always hugged Louise back. Right away Emily felt better. She knew that the "No hugging" rule for people with AIDS was silly. After meeting Louise, Emily was never again afraid to hug people she loved, even if she did have AIDS.

At Jacob's Well
John 4

This story is recorded only in the gospel of John. It is set in the context of the religious and racial rivalry of Jews and Samaritans. The focus is on the woman who was the first missionary to Samaria, although Philip is often mistakenly credited with that role.

The woman was obviously theologically trained, and knew both her religious heritage and her liturgical history. She knew about sister religions such as Judaism. She knew about the Messiah concept. Lydia Niguidula of the Philippines, in an article entitled "The Untouchable Touched" (*In God's Image*), suggests that the woman knew the triple oppression of race (she was Samaritan), sex (she was female), and class (she was probably a prostitute, forced to it because of her economically precarious position).

She would rather accept discrimination and the pain and humiliation that goes with it than protest her situation. She was prepared to put up with her life even though it meant continual oppression. Yet she longed for a change when she said, "Give me this living water."

To her great surprise, Jesus listened to her. He focused on water, a basic need of her life, and symbolic of new life and hope. He treated her as an equal and recognized her worth. Through her witness, and by her pointing people to Jesus, many Samaritans believed. For children, the point of contact might be racism and prejudice. Jesus reached out across the barriers of race and religion put up by both Jew and Samaritan. Jesus' posture is always inclusive and welcoming.

Or you might focus on water. You may wish to talk about how people in many parts of the world still get their water for cooking and drinking from wells. If the well dries up, or the water becomes "brackish," it is no good and cannot be used.

For Further Reading

Wahlberg, Rachel Conrad. "Jesus and the Women Preachers." In *Jesus According to a Woman*, New York: Paulist Press, 1975, p. 89.

At Jacob's Well

story by Beatrice Arnill,
Parry Sound, Ontario

Yellow or black,
Sikh or Jew,
Love the other
As they do you.

In the days of Jesus, there was a well in Samaria called Jacob's well. It was on the outskirts of a town called Sychar. Living in that town was a girl called Ruth. She was big for her age and full of mischief. She preferred to play outside with her cousin Joel rather than help with the housework.

"Who will ever marry a lazy obstinate girl like you?" her mother would scold. "You will grow up to be just like Rebecca."

Rebecca was a woman in the town who had no friends. The children were forbidden to go near her. When Ruth had asked why, her mother refused to answer. Being compared to a woman who had obviously committed some horrible crime hurt Ruth. But she refused to show it.

One day during the hot season Ruth and her cousin Joel were playing in a field near Jacob's well. It was midday and very hot. Looking up, Ruth saw Rebecca coming from the town to draw water. Scooping up a handful of stones she said, "Let's creep up to the well and scare Rebecca. We'll hide and throw these stones at her. She won't even know who did it." Her eyes sparkled.

"What if we get caught?"

"How? No one but Rebecca ever comes to the well at noon. It's hot. Come on."

The children crept up behind a tree close to the well. Ruth peeked around the tree. A stranger was seated at the well talking to Rebecca. She was giving him a drink of water.

"What are we going to do now," whispered Joel.

"Sh-sh," said Ruth. "They're talking about the water in the well...She's pointing to the mountain... Now Rebecca is running back to town and she left her jug. Let's go out and see what happened."

The children walked over to the well. "Hello," said the stranger who was Jesus. Ruth and Joel were suddenly struck by shyness and could say nothing.

"What is in your hand?" asked Jesus.

Ruth blushed and tried to hide them. "Stones," she mumbled.

"What are you doing with stones," asked Jesus.

"Well..." said Ruth.

"She was going to throw them at Rebecca," said Joel.

"Why?"

"Because Rebecca is a wicked woman. She deserves it," said Ruth defensively.

"She was kind and gave me a drink of water," said Jesus.

"It doesn't matter," replied Ruth. "Nobody talks to her and you shouldn't either."

Jesus reached out his hand and took the stones.

"What do you deserve," he asked.

The question took Ruth by surprise.

"I don't know," she said. "I'm not very good." Her lower lip began to tremble. "My mother says I'm lazy and obstinate and will grow up to be just like Rebecca. Then nobody will like me either." Tears spilled over and ran down her cheeks.

Jesus put her on his knee and wiped away the tears.

"I think you will grow up to be just yourself," he said kindly, "and many people will like you."

In the distance they could see Rebecca returning from town with a crowd of people. "You'd better go," said Joel. "People will be angry with you for talking to Rebecca."

But the crowd was not angry – they were curious. Rebecca had returned to the town full of excitement about the young man at Jacob's well.

"Come and see," she urged. "I know he comes from God. Who else could speak such marvelous words and tell me everything I ever did?"

So the townspeople came to see and were not disappointed. They listened and knew that here was a special man.

Jesus stayed in Sychar for two days teaching and healing people. When he left, Ruth and Joel were waiting for him at Jacob's well. Jesus stopped.

"Goodbye," he said, and gave them each a hug.